The Hallway Miracle is a gripping, heareads like a novel b
Cara Shine master:
bold, life-changing 1
inspire you to live
longing to share Ch   —buy extra
copies to place in the hands of every seeker you know.

— Carol Kent

speaker, executive director of Speak Up Ministries, and author of *When I Lay My Isaac Down*

What begins as a harrowing account of fear and tragedy unfolds into a breathtaking story of hope, faith, and God's relentless pursuit. Cara Shine's courageous vulnerability and compelling storytelling drew me in from the first page, as she shares her raw, real, and redemptive journey from fear to faith. *The Hallway Miracle* is a powerful reminder that even in our darkest hours, no one is beyond the reach of God's love and grace.

— Rachael Adams

author of *A Little Goes a Long Way* and *Everyday Prayers*, host of *The Love Offering* podcast

If you want to read a book with the fingerprint of God all over it, then this is the book you must read. If you ache to see God's presence in one person's ordinary life, then this book is the one you have been longing for. Cara Shine's book, *The Hallway Miracle*, is an amazing story of God's creativity, His unconditional love, and His relentless pursuit of humanity. Cara is the real deal, and her story is too riveting to ignore. You will feel Cara's fear during momentous days in our nation's history, but you will also embrace the peace that Cara claimed as her very own. Cara Shine's testimony is filled with grace, hope, and miracles. Be prepared to stay up all night because you won't be able to put this book down!

— Carol McLeod

speaker, podcaster, and author of *Today is a Verb, The Rooms of a Mother's Heart*, and other titles

Want a story that will grab your heart and not let go? Cara Shine has done it with *The Hallway Miracle*. From the very first page, Cara's riveting journey grips your heart. She was a Jewish wife, mother, and schoolteacher living the dream, until fear of the Beltway Snipers nearly paralyzed her with dread. You'll feel the raw anguish of a parent desperate to protect her child, the silent torment of a soul suffocating in fear, and the deep longing for peace amid chaos. But most of all, you will witness the breathtaking transformation of a woman who once knew nothing about Jesus—and came to know Him as her very best friend. Cara's testimony is a powerful reminder that no one is beyond the reach of God's grace. *The Hallway Miracle* isn't just a story—it's an invitation to hope, to healing, and to the kind of freedom only Jesus can bring. I highly recommend it to you!

— Marnie Swedberg
international leadership mentor and author

The Hallway Miracle is Cara's story, a story about how Jesus is revealed through everyday, ordinary lives. There is no parting of the sea, no burning bush, no exit from a tomb. But there is a changed life, and that is a miracle. The people in this story did not find the snipers, stop the fear, or have the answers to all life's difficult moments. They simply were themselves, trying to live a life of faith. I personally know all the participants in this story. As pastor of the church that celebrated Cara's baptism, I can attest that they are all ordinary people—no superhumans. That is the story's power. It reminds us that God works through us if we simply show up. It reminds us that a relationship with God is a process, one that continues for all our lives. And it reminds us that we all need to pay attention to those we work beside, shop beside, and live beside.

— Pastor Brian Clark
director National Capital Missional Incubator

Brave. Faithful. Anxious. God Winks. Humble. These are words that come to mind as I mentored Cara through this book-writing process. She is deeply devoted to sharing the message God has placed on her heart, despite all the obstacles. Yes, she was anxious and afraid at times, and yet God always showed up in amazing ways as she bravely followed the path that was before her. Her story shines a light on the importance for all Christians to step out of their comfort zone and tell someone about Jesus. It powerfully shows what amazing things can happen if you do. It is sad to think that Cara's story would never have happened if those around her had remained quiet. Hopefully, it will encourage you to pray for those around you and to share the message when and how the opportunity presents itself. This would make for some wonderful Bible Study discussions.

> — Michele Novotni
>> Ph.D., psychologist, coach, and author of *Angry with God*

The Hallway Miracle is a powerful, compelling invitation to life with Jesus. Cara Shine's story unfolds in the shadow of one of the most terrifying chapters in recent American history—the Beltway Sniper attacks of the early 2000s. With remarkable honesty and grace, she shares what it meant to live through that trauma and how she learned to be still in the midst of both public chaos and personal turmoil. In a world where some depictions of Jesus feel anything but loving, Cara's story stands apart. With compassion and clarity, she names the real-life barriers—racism, bullying, cultural heritage, and life circumstances—that so often keep us from the God who longs to welcome us home. With a voice that is both vulnerable and vibrant, Cara draws readers in and gently leads them to the Jesus who's been there all along. Her debut shines with the kind of freedom and faith many are still searching for.

> — Jennifer Sakata
>> speaker, author, and host of *Living the Grace Life* podcast

The Hallway Miracle

The Prayer that Opened a Jewish Heart to Jesus

Cara Shine

The Hallway Miracle:
The Prayer that Opened a Jewish Heart to Jesus
Copyright © 2026 Cara Shine

All rights reserved. No part of this publication may be reproduced, stored in a retrieval system, or transmitted in any form or by any means— electronic, mechanical, photocopying, recording, or otherwise—without prior written permission of the copyright holder, except for brief quotations used in reviews or scholarly works.

ISBN: 978-1-963377-97-2 (paperback)
ISBN: 978-1-963377-86-6 (ePub)
Library of Congress Control Number: 2026932799

Abundance Books
Kalamazoo, Michigan
www.abundance-books.com

Printed in the United States of America
10 9 8 7 6 5 4 3 2 1
Cover design by Barefaced Media
This is a memoir. The events are true to the best of the author's memory.

Scriptures marked NIV are taken from the NEW INTERNATIONAL VERSION (NIV): Scripture taken from THE HOLY BIBLE, NEW INTERNATIONAL VERSION ®. Copyright © 1973, 1978, 1984, 2011 by Biblica, Inc.™. Used by permission of Zondervan

Scriptures marked NKJV are taken from the NEW KING JAMES VERSION (NKJV): Scripture taken from the NEW KING JAMES VERSION®. Copyright © 1982 by Thomas Nelson, Inc. Used by permission. All rights reserved.

This book is dedicated to my family. Thank you for the time, space, and encouragement I needed to move this story from my soul onto paper. Your unfailing love allowed for this happy ending.

Acknowledgements

I had planned on sticking quietly to the sidelines of my home church in Northern Virginia until Dr. Michele Novotni sat in on a seminar I was teaching. Afterwards, she looked me square in the eye and said, "I think God wants me to help you." And help she did. Michele, thank you for teaching me how to be brave and to faithfully obey when God calls. This book simply wouldn't exist without you.

Thank you to Lisa Mears, my technology and creativity guru, who lived through these events with me and then became my sounding board as I wrote every chapter. Thank you also to Lisa's daughter, Katie Mears, for generously editing this book. Who could have imagined that after she was my fifth-grade student, she'd grow up and edit this book! How's that for a God Wink?

A special thank you to the steadfast ladies of my Thursday night Bible study, who held my hand every step of the way, and to my Tuesday morning high schoolers, who inspired me to take this leap of faith. A heartfelt thank you to the staff and members of Riverside Presbyterian Church, who gave me room to grow, and the organizers of the "Speak Up" conference, who gave me a community of other dreamers. And to the countless number of friends who prayed for me during this process, thank you! I could write a second book about all of the God Winks I experienced!

Contents

Acknowledgements 9

Prologue 12

Chapter One: Alarms 14

Chapter Two: "Good" Christians 21

Chapter Three: *Whoosh* 28

Chapter Four: Bullets 36

Chapter Five: Peanuts 44

Chapter Six: Warmth 49

Chapter Seven: Fear Not 51

Chapter Eight: The Prayer 55

Chapter Nine: A Mustard Seed 61

Chapter Ten: Gifts 71

Chapter Eleven: Church 78

Chapter Twelve: Matthew 88

Chapter Thirteen: Caught 93

Chapter Fourteen: Tom 95

Chapter Fifteen: Red Light 102

Chapter Sixteen: Green Light 105

Chapter Seventeen: A New Life 109

Chapter Eighteen: 20 Years Later 115

Resources 121

About the Author 125

Prologue

For three weeks in October of 2002, none of us felt safe going outside. We stopped taking our children to playgrounds, high school football games were canceled, and simple tasks like pumping gas became a matter of life or death. Instead of going on hayrides or sipping hot apple cider that fall, we hid from the rifle of a madman and his teenage accomplice.

During three weeks of hell, the Beltway Snipers paralyzed the D.C. Metro area. They turned their blue Chevrolet Caprice into a rolling instrument of evil, shooting from the trunk of their car and using their military training to elude law enforcement. Without any clear motive, they hunted men, women, and children. By the time the two snipers were finally captured on October 24th, 2002, they had killed ten, critically wounded three, and terrorized millions.

Whatever their motives were, whatever they hoped to accomplish, I'm certain of one thing—neither of them could have predicted that their bullets would cause the heart of a Jewish woman to burst wide open to receive Jesus Christ as Lord and Savior. But that's exactly what happened to me.

This salvation story isn't mine. It belongs to God and the Christians who bravely shared the gospel with me. My prayer is that somewhere in this story, you will see either yourself, a family member, a co-worker, or a friend who simply needs your compassion to walk them into the open arms of Christ.

It's been over two decades since that fall. I've done my best to recount these events as accurately as my memory allows. My sole intent with this story is to glorify God.

"You intended to harm me, but God intended it for good to accomplish what is now being done, the saving of many lives." (Genesis 50:20, NIV)

Chapter One

Alarms

My radio alarm clock woke me rudely at 5:30 a.m. I don't know why it surprised me, I was the one who had set it. I liked to play a game in my head each night, trying to guess what song might play the next morning. Today it was "Sk8er Boi," by Avril Lavigne.

I reached across the bed and hit the "off" button as quickly as I could to keep from waking my husband, Jeff, still asleep and enjoying thirty extra minutes of sleep. *Lucky*, I thought, looking at him burrowed underneath a mountain of burgundy blankets. The weather had just started to turn, and we were trying to squeak in a few extra nights without turning on the heat. He shifted under the covers, but stayed asleep, somehow immune to Avril's charm.

We'd met at a party in West Virginia in 1992, when he tapped me on the shoulder and said simply, "Hi! What are you doing here?" smiling like a Cheshire cat and making me laugh immediately, like we already shared some secret inside joke. "I guess meeting you!" I smiled back.

He was tall and muscular with dark brown eyes and a thick southern drawl. He'd grown up in a small coal mining town, deep in the mountains of Western Pennsylvania, far away from the world I knew. But something about him instantly made me feel like I'd just found my home. I laughed out loud when he told me his last name was Shine. It fit him to a T.

We spent the next few months making the three-hour drive back and forth between the campuses of Ohio State University, where I was finishing up my teaching degree, and West Virginia University, where he had just graduated and gotten a job as a bank auditor. We spent hours exploring and comparing each campus, pizza shop, mountain bike trail, and football team.

But our favorite place to be was on the small boat Jeff owned and kept on a nearby lake near the WVU campus. Before heading out, we would stop at a local gas station and load up on premade turkey sandwiches and sodas before meeting his friends down at the dock. They all spent weeks patiently trying to teach me how to water ski, and when I finally stood up, their cheers echoed off the Allegheny Mountains.

"She's a keeper, Jeff, what's she doing with you?" his college buddy Sam joked.

"Yeah, she'd be perfect if she weren't a Buckeye fan," his friend Tom teased.

And after introducing Jeff to my friends back at Ohio State, there were high-fives all around, too. "A man who finally treats you right, it's about time!"

Everything was perfect, except for one thing. I was a Jew; he was a Presbyterian. Marrying outside of my faith had never been part of my plan, but I also hadn't planned on meeting someone like Jeff. Antisemitic bullying and harassment that I suffered growing up at the hands of Christians had left scars that only deepened my commitment to Judaism, but now I was torn.

Because I loved being Jewish, I'd grown up in the synagogue, surrounded by loving people, beautiful ceremonies, and deep traditions. My family celebrated Rosh Hashanah, the Jewish New Year, by eating apples and honey in the hopes of a sweet New Year, and we fasted ten days later during Yom Kippur as we asked God to forgive our sins and inscribe us in the book of life. I attended Sunday school every week, and I listened intently as our Rabbi read verses from the Torah, Genesis, Exodus, Leviticus, Numbers, and Deuteronomy, year after year.

But my love for Jeff challenged all of that, and I felt like I had to decide: love or religion. Jeff surprised me and offered a solution I hadn't even considered.

"Why can't I just come to synagogue with you?" He asked simply. While he believed in God, he wasn't the type to go to church every week. But if this was important to me, now it was important to him, too. He even agreed that any children we might be blessed with could be raised Jewish. He hugged me tightly, and in that moment, I knew that whatever the path, we'd figure it out together. I vowed to try to be the best version of myself for him in return.

We were married by a Rabbi under a Chuppah, and Jeff stepped on the ceremonial glass with gusto as our parents cried with joy and shouted, "Mazel Tov!" Tom and Sam lifted our chairs so high during the traditional Hora dance, they almost launched us through the ceiling, as the guests circled around us singing "Hava Nagilah." Jeff smiled from ear to ear, making me proud to be Mrs. Cara Shine.

Jeff sold his boat when he landed a job at a large bank in Northern Virginia, just outside of Washington, D.C., and I secured my dream job as a fifth-grade teacher at a nearby school, Algonkian Elementary, nestled right next to the Potomac River. We settled into the rhythms of married life in suburbia, learning and growing together. Seven years in and still no itch in sight.

Chapter One: Alarms

"Shoot," I mumbled to myself, struggling to reach a shoe on the top shelf of my dark closet, trying to get ready for school as quietly as I could. I looked around for something I could use to shimmy the shoe closer to the edge. I settled on a wire hanger that I bent into a makeshift hook. I was feeling proud of my MacGyver ingenuity, inching the shoe closer to my fingertips until the shoe slipped off past my hand and landed with a loud thud on the floor. I peeked around the door into the bedroom to see if I'd woken Jeff up. From under the covers, I heard him laugh.

"Time to make the doughnuts," he said, climbing out of bed. He woke up happy every morning, the antidote to my alarm clock.

As much as I hated the alarm part of my morning, I loved what came next. Waking up our sweet, two-year old daughter, Emma Kate, to get her ready for the day.

I stepped quietly into the hallway, the morning sun leading a path to her bedroom, and gently pushed the door open. We'd painted the walls of her bedroom pink and green, and it made me happy just to stand there, Berenstain Bear books and toys strewn across the carpet.

We'd just moved her from her crib into a big girl bed that she loved, mostly because now she could tiptoe down the hallway in the middle of the night for extra snuggles. And this morning, poking out at the top of the bed, I could see her head on the pillow, a mess of tousled, soft brown curls, just like her daddy. Her arms were wrapped around her blankie—innocent, safe, and protected. I could feel the warmth of her skin under my hand as I gently roused her awake.

Emma's first word wasn't Mama or Dada, it was "ball." She threw her first ball at ten months, nearly taking my head off in the process. Jeff was over the moon when he arrived home from work that day to discover we'd given birth to an athlete. They played ball almost every day as soon as he got home from work. She kept us busy, never wanting to sit down, voraciously curious, and growing up way too fast for my liking.

We had our morning routine down pat: brush her teeth, pick out her clothes, and then pancakes or waffles for breakfast. Then Emma and I would give Jeff a kiss goodbye before heading to Mrs. Susan's house, half a mile away from my school. I'd taught Mrs. Susan's daughter, Rachel, the year before and when Susan heard I was pregnant, she jumped at the chance to cuddle a baby again. I'm not sure who loved Mrs. Susan more, Emma or me.

I checked my rearview mirror to see Emma smiling back at me as we sang her favorite song, a classic from The Wiggles, "Fruit Salad," as we drove to school that morning. The sky was gray and it was cold enough for her fleece jacket. We loved watching the sunrises on our early morning drives to Mrs. Susan's house, but this morning, the sun stayed hidden.

Now a sixth grader in middle school, Rachel was always the first to answer the door in the morning when I dropped Emma off, her older sister Allison and father Doug usually right behind, laughing, chasing, and loving Emma as if she were their own. I gave Emma a big squeeze and watched her run into the house to play with Hunter, their beloved Labrador. Even though I knew she was safe and loved, my heart hurt every time I left her.

As I pulled away from the house, I switched the radio station from the Disney Channel to the news. The news cycle was focused on the hunt for Osama Bin Laden and the ongoing war in Iraq. It had barely been a year since 9/11 and I couldn't help but think about that day all over again.

Rachel had been in my fifth-grade class the day the planes hit the Twin Towers. News spread quickly between teachers, but we were instructed not to share anything with our

Chapter One: Alarms

students. Instead, we had to carry on teaching as if nothing had happened, even though all the students could sense something was very wrong. Many of them had parents who worked at the Pentagon, just twenty miles away from our Northern Virginia suburb, but all we could do as teachers was to repeat the one sentence our principal, Rob Duckworth, had given us: "Something has happened in our country, but you are safe here with me at school. Your parents will explain everything to you when you get home."

I hated that I had to repeat that line, "You are safe here with me," because in all honesty, I had no idea if I could keep anyone safe. I had to jam my hands into my pockets so my students couldn't see that they were shaking.

And nearly a year later, like many Americans, I was still on edge. But not Jeff. He decided he wasn't going to live in fear, worrying about every little thing. He relied on the same "country strong" confidence he'd used to steer his beloved boat through rocky waters. He carried on as if nothing had changed. He made it look so easy, but for me, it felt like an uphill battle.

My parents could sense my unrest. "Cara, why don't you try again to find a nice synagogue?" they suggested. Jeff and I had tried a few when we had first moved to Virginia, and again after Emma had been born, and while they were full of the same beautiful traditions I'd grown up with, none of them felt like home. I longed for the same closeness I'd felt to God growing up, but now it felt strangely out of reach. And so, after a few years, we stopped going at all.

A few errant raindrops on my car's windshield snapped me back into reality as I made the final right-hand turn into school. I had a classroom full of fifth graders who needed me to teach them how to master long division. I didn't have time to think about 9/11 or synagogues anymore.

The parking lot was filling up quickly as students piled out of buses and into school, and I parked my maroon Honda Accord in one of the last open spots. I grabbed my cup of coffee and oversized teacher bag and headed into school, just as the alarm bell rang out; no "Sk8er Boi" playing in the background this time.

Chapter Two

"Good" Christians

I sped up my pace and maneuvered through the hallway, now full of kids who were also speedwalking so they could be first to their classroom. Being "first" was the driving force behind almost everything my fifth graders did. First to the classroom, first to raise their hand, first to lunch, and, the most coveted of all the firsts, first in line. It always made me smile, as did almost everything else they did. As hard as teaching was—juggling the needs of twenty-eight little humans and their parents, trying to plan dynamic lessons, and grading papers late into the night—I still wouldn't have traded it for anything.

I tried to make a sharp cut through the mob of kids, but a determined, red-headed first grader with a rolling Spiderman backpack suddenly jumped in front of me. I hit the brakes, tumbled into a wall, and spilled my coffee all over my pants.

"Sorry," came his little voice as he looked down at me, scared he was about to be in big trouble.

"Oh honey, it's okay," I said, "Don't worry, just slow down, okay?" I tried not to let my annoyance show.

As I lay on the ground in a heap, I heard the familiar southern drawl of my work bestie, Sharon. "Girl, maybe you should slow down! Are you okay?" she asked, dripped in both concern and laughter. She reached out her hand and pulled me up off the floor.

Sharon was a seasoned teacher and everybody's friend. She was tall with wavy auburn hair and hazel eyes and possessed that "it" factor, making her both a magnet for fun and a shoulder to cry on. I was certain she'd never met a stranger in her life. On my first day at Algonkian, she invited me to sit with her in the teacher's lounge, introducing me to everyone and instantly making me feel part of the team. Her classroom was just across the hall from mine, which meant we also relied on each other for the most important task of all: bathroom breaks.

"Well, that was messy," I laughed as she helped scoop me off the hallway floor.

"Messy?" Sharon squinted at me. "What's messy is that coffee stain all over your pants. Come into my room real quick, I have a Tide Stick in my drawer, I bet we can get most of it out before the kids even hang up their backpacks."

Walking into Sharon's classroom was like walking straight into a hug. There were soft bean bag chairs for a reading nook, lush green plants growing on the windowsill, and a guinea pig named Caramel that her kids took home on the weekends.

"I know it's in one of these drawers," she said, rummaging through paperclips and Post-it pads, knocking over a small, triangular, stand-up desk calendar in the process. I reached down to fix it. Each page had a date and what I assumed were inspirational quotes. I flipped it back to the date for today, October 2nd, and read the page.

> Jesus conquered death so that you could live! He didn't die a sinner's death so that fear would rule over your life. Choose joy every day and never forget how much you are loved by the King!

Chapter Two: "Good" Christians

"Fear not, for I am with you; Be not dismayed, for I am your God. I will strengthen you, Yes, I will help you, I will uphold you with My righteous right hand." (Isaiah 41:10 NKJV)

This was a daily devotional of Bible verses meant for Christians, something I knew wasn't meant for me, a Jew.

Sharon's head popped up from under the piles as she thrust the Tide Stick triumphantly into the air, "Found it!"

I felt as if I'd just read something I wasn't supposed to, something intimate, like Sharon's diary. I redirected my gaze. Her eyes softened as she caught my glance, and she smiled. She looked at me as if she wanted to say something, but I didn't give her the time. Her Christian calendar made me uncomfortable. I took the Tide Stick and awkwardly turned toward the door.

"Thanks, Sharon, you're the best! I'll bring the stick back after lunch!" I called back over my shoulder. I turned quickly and headed out of her room and into the hallway, still thinking how odd it was that she had something so religious on her desk and in plain sight. I shook off the thought and walked into my classroom.

"Morning, everybody!" I said cheerfully.

"Morning, Mrs. Shine," they said, many of them still trying to get organized and unpack their backpacks.

"Guess what we're doing today?" I asked them.

"Getting extra recess?" a few asked hopefully.

"Better! We're practicing long division." I smiled, knowing their groans in response were good-hearted. As the last of them took their seats, the morning announcements began.

"Goooooood mooooooorning Algonkian Bobcats!" came the enthusiastic voice of our principal, Mr. Rob Duckworth, over the loudspeaker. The shuffling of school supplies stopped.

The kids didn't want to miss a word of what Mr. Duckworth might say. A family man with soft brown eyes, a wide smile, and an infectious laugh, Rob wasn't a stereotypical principal. Rather than bending his staff with an iron will, he empowered us to be the best versions of ourselves. Our high test scores reflected his leadership. When Emma needed to be rushed to the pediatrician's office at the beginning of the school year for some sort of reaction that caused her eye to swell, Rob stepped in and covered my class so I could be with her. "Family always comes first," was his motto.

I heard rumors that after the staff had gone home, he would walk the hallways, reaching out and touching each door to pray for each of us. I had never heard of such a thing. His open display of spirituality shocked me at first, but it was hard to deny his genuineness, even if we didn't share the same theology. He was, I decided, a good Christian man. A rare thing because up until that point, Christians had done far more harm than good to my family.

Growing up in a small, Southwestern suburb of Ohio in the 1970's, we were one of the only Jewish families in an otherwise very Christian community. The only synagogue we could find was forty minutes away, and most of our neighbors had never met a Jew before. To them, we must have seemed like foreigners. We ate exotic foods like bagels and spread our peanut butter and jelly on Matzo crackers instead of Wonderbread.

Before my brother and I started elementary school, my mom and dad met with the principal to develop a plan to protect us from potential antisemitism. Together, they decided that sharing a few of our Jewish traditions and inserting one traditional Jewish song into the annual Christmas play might be a good idea. But it only seemed to have the opposite effect. Sitting in music class, as the teacher announced, "Today we're learning a traditional Jewish folk song for the Christmas play," I could feel the eyes and hear the disapproving whispers of some of my classmates who echoed what they'd heard at home. "This is a Christmas play, not a Hanukkah play."

But my mom refused to give up, and she dedicated herself to helping us fit in. She decided she would throw Hanukkah parties for our classmates each year. She would bring in a portable skillet and cook homemade potato latkes for everyone, complete with sweet applesauce, tangy sour cream, and chives. Our classmates would huddle around her and watch as each pancake sizzled and fried in the hot oil, the edges popping and then turning a deep golden brown.

Those were some of the good days. But many of the rest were hard, especially on the school bus. With no one to protect us, kids were free to say or do whatever they wanted. Once, an older "Christian" boy walked past me, grabbed a handful of my hair, and proudly announced to the entire bus, "Checked her for horns! All clear!" And the day another child asked, "Do you like warm weather? Cause it's going to be really hot in Hell." Or a personal favorite of a blonde-headed girl, "My dad says your family must be ignorant since you don't believe in Jesus Christ." She would punctuate and hiss the words, "Jesus Christ," almost spitting them at me. The name sounded so ugly coming out of her mouth. I would sink as low as I could into my seat, making myself as small as possible. I always wondered why no one spoke up to defend us, since I was certain that not everyone on that bus agreed with these bullies. But no one ever did.

The ironic part was that we were never taught anything hateful about Jesus in synagogue. In fact, we heard that he was a Rabbi and teacher who preached the Golden Rule, "Do unto others as you would have them do unto you." I couldn't reconcile this Jesus with the hateful and damning version of Him that the kids on the bus seemed to know. But Rob and Sharon seemed different, and I wondered how they'd turned out that way.

Mr. Duckworth continued with the morning announcements, "As we begin another day, let us pause for a minute of silence." State-mandated after 9/11, all students and staff were required to stop whatever they were doing for an entire minute of introspection or maybe even prayer. I usually fidgeted my way through the "minute of silence," rolling a rubber band or paper clip between my thumb and forefinger, my mind already focused on the million things I had to do that day. My students followed suit and usually did the same.

After a very long minute, Mr. Duckworth broke the spell, and we all rose to recite the Pledge of Allegiance. "I pledge allegiance to the flag of the United States of America. One Nation, under God…" Under God? My mind wandered back to Sharon's Christian desk calendar.

The rest of the day went by uneventfully, and after the dismissal bell rang, I stayed an extra hour getting my classroom and lesson plans ready for the next day. I picked Emma up around 4:30 p.m., and we headed to the grocery store to grab a few things for dinner.

I was distracted as I pushed Emma around the grocery store aisles, her legs dangling through the shopping cart seat that I had meticulously wiped down with Lysol wipes beforehand. I decided to make chicken parmesan for dinner and grabbed all the ingredients I needed, along with a treat for Emma, a pack of M&M's. I paid for our groceries, packed everything into the car, and snapped her back into her car seat. I couldn't wait to throw on my baggy sweats, wash my face, and finally relax, just the three of us at home.

I made the left-hand turn out of the grocery store parking lot to head home when I realized the radio was still tuned to the news station from this morning. I was just about to change it back to the Disney Channel for another round of The Wiggles when I heard the breaking news.

There had been a strange shooting in Aspen Hill, Maryland. Shots had been fired into a local Michael's craft store

Chapter Two: "Good" Christians

window at 5:20 p.m. I turned the station quickly so Emma wouldn't hear, not that she would understand anyway, but I wanted to protect her.

I had grown accustomed to hearing about the violence that often came with living outside of Washington, D.C., but shots being fired into a craft store was unusual. My shoulders tensed.

Chapter Three

Whoosh

As Emma and I made the final turn into our neighborhood, I could see a gaggle of kids playing basketball at my neighbor Sheku's house. Emma adored Sheku and clamored to get out of her car seat so she could play, too. I abandoned the groceries in my car to steal a few minutes alone with Sheku while the kids played.

Sheku's smile lit up her face, which wasn't hard since she had both the personality and natural beauty of a Pakistani queen. She was the first to welcome Jeff and me to the neighborhood when we moved in, arriving at our doorstep with a warm bowl of saffron and chickpea rice that made my mouth water just thinking about it.

I admired the detailed, bronze-colored henna on her hands, leftover from a wedding she'd been to that weekend. We chatted and caught up as we watched the children chasing each other around the yard.

"You wouldn't have believed the bride's dress!" Sheku exclaimed. "It was the most stunning color of red! It was to die for!"

"And the food?" I teased, hoping she'd offer me a few bites

Chapter Three: Whoosh

of the leftovers I was certain she had tucked inside her refrigerator.

"You know I brought some home!" she giggled. "Come over when you're free, and we can sit in my sunroom and eat it all!" I quietly thought about how unique our friendship was. A Jew and a Muslim, united by a deep friendship just outside the nation's Capital. I thought about bringing up the news of the shooting, but decided against it.

Right on time, Jeff arrived home from work. He parked his car, grabbed a few grocery bags out of my car, and then made a beeline for Emma. She abandoned her game of chase and ran as fast as her two-year-old legs could carry her, jumping into his arms. He juggled both her and the groceries inside as Sheku and I said goodnight and promised we would have a sunroom session soon.

Emma was already busy playing with a set of handmade wooden blocks that my dad made by the time I got inside. Jeff was busy putting away the groceries. I knew my first words to him should have been something like, "How was your day?" but I couldn't stop myself.

"Did you hear about that shooting?"

"Yeah," he said as he helped put the groceries away. "It's all over the news. They said there was a second shooting in Wheaton a few minutes ago in a grocery store parking lot. I think the guy died."

Jeff clocked the fear on my face. "Relax, I'm sure they'll figure it out," he stated calmly.

Relax. I detested that word. I envied everything about his ability to stay relaxed in almost every situation.

My cheeks started to feel hot, but Emma's voice rang out throughout the kitchen. She had grown tired of the wooden blocks and jumped up and down, pulling on Jeff's hand as she begged, "Outside, Daddy! Let's play ball outside!"

Jeff shrugged his shoulders as he looked at her defenselessly, "What Lil' Em wants, Lil' Em gets," as they headed out the back door.

I turned to the pile of ingredients and hoped they would somehow magically turn themselves into chicken parmesan. The kitchen was too quiet without them, so I turned on the television. Local news reporters were giving updates on the shootings. I turned my attention to the eggs I was cracking.

"Ugh," I muttered as I accidentally let a few shells fall into the bowl. I grabbed a knife to try to fish them out.

"James D. Martin, a program analyst for the National Oceanic and Atmospheric Administration, was fatally shot while loading his groceries into his car," the reporter said. "This, along with a random shooting into a Michael's craft store down the road, has local authorities on edge tonight."

The Bible verse from Sharon's desk suddenly found me again, startling me out of my train of thought. *Fear not, for I am with you*...what was the rest of the verse? I couldn't remember. *Fear not, for I am with you*. What did that even mean? Was it a command, like clean your room, and while you're at it, fear not! I wished I could command myself to be calmer, like Jeff.

All James Martin had done was go to get groceries just like Emma and I had done half an hour ago. I stared at the bowl of broken egg yolks in front of me. Maybe James had gotten the same ingredients we had gotten. I pictured James in his kitchen, preparing dinner for his family. My throat began to tighten at the thought of the empty seat left behind at his family kitchen table.

I looked out the window to watch Jeff and Emma still playing in the backyard. They chased after a mini pink soccer ball, a gift from Jeff's friend Tom, for Emma at her first birthday party. Jeff scooped her up and twirled her high into the air as she giggled with delight.

Chapter Three: Whoosh

Suddenly, without warning, a dark and sinister thought shook me: *You're going to lose them.* I froze. The room began to sway, and I was suddenly aware of my own heartbeat. I dropped the knife into the kitchen sink as a loud WHOOSH reverberated in my ear.

I grabbed the edges of the kitchen sink to steady myself, but the sound in my ears only grew louder. I turned on the water faucet, cupped my hands, and splashed cold water over my face, but the sinister thought found me again: *You're going to lose them.* I looked up and saw Jeff and Emma, still outside, laughing and playing. I wanted them inside the house with me. Now. I pounded the window with my fist to get Jeff's attention.

Jeff looked up, tilted his head, and squinted to try to make sense of what he was seeing: his wife, motioning frantically for him to come inside, presumably for dinner. He scooped Emma up and headed leisurely inside.

I tried to steady myself, but the dark thought wouldn't let me. I knew I only had seconds before they walked through the door, and I didn't want them to see me this way. I desperately wanted to be strong for both Jeff and Emma, to *relax*, like Jeff had said. The perfect wife and mother. I moved away from the sink and sat down at the table, taking long, deep breaths to steady myself. Emma came bounding through the door first, running right past me to her wooden blocks.

"Is dinner ready?" Jeff asked, looking confused by the empty dinner table. Just being in the room with them slowed my heart rate down. The *whoosh* faded as quickly as it had begun.

"Everything okay?" he asked.

"Yeah, I'm fine," I lied. "I just got lightheaded for a second. I feel better now."

Jeff looked at me, squinting his eyes, trying to figure out what he'd missed. "You sure you're okay?" he asked again.

"Yeah, yeah," I dismissed him, standing up quickly to prove my point. *See, you can relax when you try hard enough,* I thought. "Let me finish dinner, and we can eat in a few minutes," I said, walking back to the pile of ingredients.

I picked up a clean knife and returned to making dinner, my hands still shaking slightly. I focused on each task, dredging the chicken in the eggs and then into the breadcrumbs.

By the time dinner was finally ready, I felt steadier. Jeff buckled Emma into her booster seat and tucked her bib around her neck. The phone rang suddenly, causing me to jump and Emma to giggle. Jeff crossed the room to pick up the phone.

"Hello?" he answered, "Hey, Tom!" He grinned, letting his Pennsylvania drawl fly. "What's up, buddy?"

Emma and I both broke out into wide smiles at the mention of Tom's name.

"Tom! Tom! Tom!" Emma sang loudly enough for Tom to hear as she kicked her little legs in excitement.

"I think someone wants to say hi to you, Tom," said Jeff, holding the phone to Emma's ear so she could hear him. Her face lit up. I guess we all felt that way about Tom—his friendship meant everything to us. He was tall, blond, and exceedingly witty. He may have been Jeff's friend first, but I loved him like a brother. Memories of him jumping into the water as I learned to water ski on Jeff's boat made me smile.

Just like Jeff, after Tom graduated from WVU, he moved to D.C. to take a job working on Capitol Hill. Reunited once again, and before Emma had even been born, we spent every weekend exploring our new city, working our first real jobs, and making lots of trips back to WVU to cheer on the Mountaineers.

I'd taught Tom how to make a good lasagna, and he'd taught me his mom's famous spaghetti alla puttanesca sauce. And when Tom was suddenly diagnosed with Type 1 Diabetes, we all had to learn how to give him an emergency shot of glucose in case his blood sugar ever fell too low.

But all of our weekend fun came to a halt when Tom suddenly announced that he'd taken a new job as a marketing executive for tobacco powerhouse Philip Morris in New York City. We were all devastated. No one wanted to break up the friend group, but it was simply too good an opportunity for him to pass up.

"You're leaving us for big tobacco, Tom? Do you really have to?" I pleaded.

"Somebody has to keep the big boys honest, right?" He laughed as he packed all of his belongings into his car. I cried as he pulled away.

But his phone calls helped to keep our bonds tight. He wanted to make sure that Emma wouldn't forget him either.

Emma jabbered over the phone. "Tom, you come play?" she asked sweetly.

"I'm sorry, Em," I heard him say through the speaker, using his best uncle voice. "I can't play today, but I'll try to come for a visit really soon, and we can go to the park and swing, Ok?"

"Ok," Em said sadly. I distracted her with the last bit of noodles left on her tray as Jeff took the phone and walked down the hallway to the study so he and Tom could discuss WVU's chances against Pitt this season.

I looked back at Emma. The tomato sauce had left deep, red stains all around her mouth.

"Em, guess what time it is? Bath time!" I announced. She squealed, clapped her hands high above her head, and shimmied out of her seat. Chicken parmesan remnants scattered everywhere.

I filled the tub with warm, soapy water and deposited her into a cloud of bubbles. I washed her head of curls and scrubbed the tomato stains off her face as she splashed and played with her plastic toys. And in the safety of her small bathroom, watching her so content, I finally did feel *relaxed*. I let out a deep sigh.

Once bathtime was over, I wrapped her in a warm, pink bathrobe and Dora the Explorer jammies, as we settled in for her bedtime stories. She demanded at least two books each night, with The Berenstain Bears on heavy rotation. Jeff and I took turns reading each night, but tonight I wanted to be the one to read to her.

She made her selections, got under the covers, and cradled herself into the crook of my arm. Her hair was still a little damp and smelling of oatmeal shampoo, prescribed by our doctor to keep her eczema in check. We finished book number two as she snuggled deeper into the blankets. She looked up at me, her brown eyes heavy, and said quietly, "Love you, Mommy." My heart exploded.

I kissed her on the forehead, backed out of the room slowly, and said, "I love you more, Em."

But as I moved into the hallway, the ominous thought resurfaced: *You're going to lose her.* I gripped the doorknob tightly, willing the thought away as my heart began to beat loudly again.

Emma rolled over to the other side of her bed and curled into a tiny ball, falling fast asleep. I backed away quietly, trying to take deep breaths. *Pull it together,* I thought. *Relax. You're acting crazy.*

I needed to see Jeff. He'd calm me down. I walked quickly toward our bedroom. He was already in bed, having finished the last of his work emails and watching television. A pile of ungraded math papers sat inside my teacher bag downstairs, but I didn't have the energy to look at them tonight. I'd deal with them tomorrow. I changed into my pajamas, peeled back the heavy burgundy comforter on our bed, and crawled inside, shoving the dark thought away.

"What do you want to watch?" he asked.

"Whatever," I said. "It doesn't matter to me."

He clicked the remote mindlessly until the local news caught his attention. "Authorities are still searching for suspects or motives surrounding today's shootings," said the anchor. "Terrorism has not been ruled out."

The sound in my ears began to build again, *WHOOSH*. I sat up suddenly, tugging on my ear to try to clear the sound. "Do you hear that?" I asked.

He looked at me, confused. "What sound?"

I thought about telling him about the haunting thought or even just the verse from Sharon's desk calendar, but I decided against it. "I guess I'm just tired," I lied. "I have a lot of papers to grade."

"Just give them all 'A's!" he laughed. "Come over here, let's watch Seinfeld instead." He adjusted his arm to make space for me to lie next to him. He laughed out loud at something Elaine and George were arguing about on the television, but all I could think about was James Martin and the "Fear Not" verse from Sharon's desk calendar. I decided to close my eyes for just a second, and before I knew it, I was fast asleep.

Chapter Four

Bullets

"Jenny from the Block," by Jennifer Lopez, blasted through the alarm clock, waking me suddenly. I reached over, turned it off, and dragged myself out of bed as Jeff shifted, but fell back asleep. I sat on the edge of the bed for just a moment, checking my heart rate and listening for any type of sound in my ear. Thankfully, there was none. Just to be safe, I kept my brain busy with the lyrics from "Jenny from the Block," as I got ready. But a slight tremor in my hand wouldn't let me forget. My mascara wand slipped and left a dark black line across my right eyelid. I grabbed a Q-tip and wiped it away.

I kept the music going in my head as I made my way down the hallway to wake Emma, who was already sitting up and waiting for me to open her door.

"Morning, Mommeeee! I hungry!" She jumped off the bed and ran into my arms.

"Ok, Em! You can eat after you get dressed and brush your teeth," I smiled. I dressed her in her favorite outfit, a long-sleeved shirt with red flowers and soft fleece black leggings. We headed downstairs for pancakes just as Jeff woke up and headed for the shower.

Chapter Four: Bullets

"Morning!" he yelled from the top of the steps. "Is everyone ok this morning?"

"Yes, Daddy," Emma yelled back, but I knew his question was really meant for me.

"Yep, all good," I smiled, giving him a thumbs up from the bottom of the steps.

"Good! Ok, I'm going to go get ready, have a good day."

"Love you, Daddy," Emma said, blowing him a kiss that he caught dramatically, making her burst out in laughter.

I threw my lunch box into my bag and gathered everything I needed for the day as Emma's hand reached up and grabbed mine.

"Mommy, I have M&M's at Sue Sue's house?" she half-asked, half-demanded, shaking the bag of M&M's like maracas. How could I say no?

"Ok, Em," I said. "But don't eat them all. Save some for tomorrow, ok?"

"Ok, Mommy," she said, grinning just like her daddy. We walked out to the car and she scrambled into her car seat.

As we turned out of the neighborhood, the sun was just beginning to rise over the Blue Ridge Mountains. I had to lower my visor to keep from being blinded. From the backseat, Emma squealed with delight. "Mommy! Woooook! It's bweeatifull!"

I tilted the visor to see that the sky had exploded into a thousand shades of pink as the sun made its grand entrance. Through the rear-view mirror, I caught the delight in Emma's eyes. I made a silent vow to do everything in my power to keep her safe, always. I gripped the steering wheel a little bit tighter as I turned onto Susan's street. We walked hand in hand up to Susan's porch, and I held our hug for a second longer than usual before watching her toddle down the hallway in search of Hunter.

As I drove to school, I made a list in my head of all the things I needed to accomplish, including grading the papers I hadn't gotten to the night before. I made a conscious decision not to think about James Martin. I simply didn't have the time.

My class was scheduled for Art every Thursday morning, which meant I started my day with a free period that I could use to make copies, plan, and grade papers. I walked into school determined to get it all done this morning. But when I grabbed my teacher bag to retrieve the ungraded papers, I saw the Tide Stick Sharon had lent me the day before lying at the bottom of the bag.

"Shoot," I said out loud, and made a beeline to Sharon's room to return it.

As usual, Sharon's kids were already on-task, organized, and working on the writing prompt Sharon had written on the board, "Tell me about the best meal you've ever eaten."

"Chicken parmesan that magically makes itself?" I said out loud to the room. My joke fell flat as Sharon's class stared at me blankly.

From across the room at her desk, Sharon chuckled, "Ha! Mrs. Shine thinks she's a comedian this morning, kids!" Her eyes were sparkling as she laughed. I held up the Tide Stick and walked over to her desk just as Rob began the announcements.

"As we begin another day, let us pause for a minute of silence."

Ugh, I was stuck. Stuck at Sharon's desk, but with no paper clip or rubber band to occupy me this time. I looked around for something to distract myself. And that's when I noticed it. One by one, many of Sharon's students closed their eyes, folded their hands, and bowed their heads. A different kind of silence spread across the room. I turned to Sharon to

Chapter Four: Bullets

see if she saw all of this too, but our eyes didn't meet. They couldn't meet, because hers were closed as well.

I felt deeply uncomfortable. The minute of silence felt more like an hour as I stood there awkwardly, counting the seconds. I searched for something to do, something to focus on. My eyes landed on Sharon's Christian desk calendar and the verse for the day.

"When the world around you seems to be swirling and out of control, take heart! Your house is built on the firm foundation that is Jesus! That doesn't mean that life will always be perfect, but you can rest in the arms of God knowing that nothing can separate you from the love of Jesus."

"Peace I leave with you; my peace I give you. I do not give to you as the world gives. Do not let your hearts be troubled and do not be afraid." (John 14:27 NIV)

This was not a book from the Torah—this was from the New Testament, a book meant for Christians, and one I'd never touched. I wondered silently about who this man John was. I reread the verse several times as Sharon and her class kept their eyes closed and heads bowed. "Do not be afraid." Another command just like the "Fear not" verse from yesterday. I wondered if these commands held some secret power that might stop the tremor in my hand or the sound in my ear.

"This concludes the minute of silence," came Rob's voice over the loudspeaker, and before I could look away, Sharon opened her eyes, catching me staring at the calendar.

She reached over and picked it up, smiling broadly. "I love this little calendar. I actually just bought it for myself! It helps me start my day right each morning. Do you want to look at it?" she asked hesitantly.

I wanted to pick up the calendar and read the Bible verses again. I wanted to ask Sharon where the verses had come from, who John was, and, more importantly, I wanted to ask if these words helped her to relax. But the face of the blonde-haired girl and other kids on the bus, hissing the name of Jesus, clamped my mouth shut.

Suddenly, there was a commotion in the hallway. Sharon and I both looked up and saw several teachers running down the hallway. We looked at each other, knowing something was wrong. Teachers never ran in the hallway.

"I'll go see what's going on," I said softly, not wanting to frighten her kids. "I'll be right back." I left her room and walked quickly down the hallway. It felt eerily like 9/11 all over again, rushing to the front office for answers. My heart began to beat faster.

A large crowd had gathered in the office. I knew immediately that something was very wrong; the television was on. The television was rarely on, not even after school hours. I wasn't even sure it worked until last year when we'd all huddled in the same place, watching in shock as the Twin Towers fell.

"Three different shootings? Already three dead?" someone gasped.

I moved closer to the television and saw a reporter on the scene at a gas station with police sirens wailing behind her in the distance.

"Authorities are issuing a warning to all residents this morning. Police are investigating three fatal shootings at three different locations. They are reporting that at approximately 7:40 a.m. this morning, a man was fatally shot while mowing the lawn outside of Fitzgerald Auto Mall. Then, thirty minutes later, at approximately 8:12 a.m., a second man was fatally shot while pumping gas here in Aspen Hill. And approximately fifteen minutes after that, a third victim, we believe a woman, was shot and killed while sitting on a bench in Silver Spring."

Chapter Four: Bullets

The crowd of teachers all started speaking at once.

"What is going on?"

"Is it one person doing all the shooting or a group?"

The reporter put her hand over her earpiece and paused as she listened for live updates. A deep furrow formed between her eyes. "I'm getting new information that there has just been a fourth shooting. Police are on the scene at a second gas station down the road. First responders are reporting another possible fatality."

More gasps and murmurs spread through the group. I thought about James Martin.

The reporter continued, "Authorities are urging the public to remain vigilant and alert. If anyone has information about any of these shootings, please contact your local police station."

"What is this world coming to? You can't even walk outside anymore without getting shot?" a teacher lamented. I thought of Emma and Susan on their daily walk with Hunter and immediately felt nauseous. And where was Jeff today? Was he in his office in Herndon or downtown in D.C. doing business? I couldn't remember.

A hush settled across the room. Our eyes moved aimlessly around, searching for answers or comfort. As if on cue, Rob stepped calmly forward.

"Whatever this is, it's out of our control. The only thing we can control is what is happening in our classrooms right now. Let's focus on our students and pray for each victim and their families. Don't be afraid."

Don't be afraid? The same words I'd just read from Sharon's Bible calendar? It was an obvious coincidence, but something deep in my chest didn't want it to be.

"I'll keep you updated," Rob reassured us. "Let's all head back to class now," he said.

I dreaded having to tell Sharon, but turned and headed back towards her classroom. I tried to harness some of Rob's calmness, but I could feel the tremor in my hand return. Other teachers began peaking their heads out of their classrooms to see what was going on, as news of the shootings spread quickly.

Sharon's smile melted as soon as she saw my face. We stepped out into the hallway so I could tell her everything. Her eyes grew wide as I described it all, and waited for her to react. She closed her eyes for a long minute, looking sad and lost, and then, just like Rob, seemed to harness a sense of calm.

"God is in control," she said confidently. "We don't have to be afraid."

I cocked my head and squinted at her. God is in control? Don't be afraid? Did she and Rob have matching desk calendars? What was going on? And judging by the past twenty-four hours, God was most definitely not in control. Where was God this morning when four innocent people were gunned down? Where had God been when James Martin was gunned down yesterday?

Sharon paused for a moment, choosing her next words carefully. "Do you want to pray with me?" she asked tentatively.

I thought about my home synagogue filled with people I loved, standing together and reciting the *Shema*, the most important prayer of my people. "Hear, O Israel: the Lord is our God; the Lord is one."

I doubted that her Christian prayer could feel the same. No, I didn't want to pray with her.

"I have to get back to my kids, Art is almost over," I said. I could see a sadness in her eyes, but I didn't care. I wanted no part of her prayer.

Chapter Four: Bullets

But just as I turned away, I saw Rob walking hurriedly towards both of us, a concerned look on his face. Had there been more shootings? Were there more deaths? I braced myself, but nothing could have prepared me for what he said next.

"Cara," he looked at me intently. "Susan just called. Something is wrong with Emma."

Chapter Five

Peanuts

"It must have been the M&M's," said the doctor. "They have traces of peanuts in them and, according to your babysitter, that was the last thing she ate before her nap. Her airway could have easily closed while she was sleeping. To be honest, you're both lucky she's alive." I bit the inside of my mouth to keep from crying in front of Emma or Jeff. I pulled Emma closer, her tiny frame weak and exhausted from the trauma. The room seemed to grow smaller and tighter.

The pale fluorescent lighting of the examination room highlighted her swollen eyes, along with the scratches on her face left behind from her tiny fingernails. The large doses of medicine they'd administered as soon as we arrived had worked quickly, but the swelling would take hours to disappear. Jeff left work to meet us at the doctor's office, and Rob had stayed with my class so I could be with Emma.

"Mr. and Mrs. Shine," the doctor said in a foreboding tone, "Emma needs to undergo further testing to see what else she might be allergic to, but in the meantime, I'm going to give you a prescription for an EpiPen. Fill it in today. She should never go anywhere without it. Anaphylaxis happens within minutes and is often fatal. Without her EpiPen, she could easily die." It felt as if the room began to tilt under my feet. I tried to focus on a red and black poster on the opposing wall with instructions on how to dial 911.

The doctor wrote out the prescription, handed it to us, and instructed us to wait for the nurse who would show us how to remove the orange safety cap on the Epi-Pen before plunging it into Emma's little thigh when she had her next reaction. The word "when" felt like a gut punch.

After another hour of observation, we were finally discharged but were given strict instructions to watch her vigilantly over the next few hours in case she had a rebound reaction. I wondered if I'd ever be able to stop watching her vigilantly.

Jeff cradled Emma in his arms as we headed back through the waiting area. I glanced at a mother wiping her toddler's runny nose, silently wishing that something as simple as over-the-counter cold medicine could cure my daughter of a life-threatening allergy.

I held the exit door open for Jeff so he could focus on carrying Emma to the car. The smile I was used to was absent from his face, and he was silent. We were both startled by the dark sky and drop in temperature; we'd been there for hours. Jeff pulled Emma closer to his chest to keep her warm as I fumbled to find the car keys, finally opening the door so he could tuck her into her car seat. She fell asleep as soon as we pulled away.

I sat perfectly still, trying to focus on the billions of stars that were visible in the cloudless sky, as I pictured Emma's new "peanut-free" life. As a teacher, I knew all too well what having a peanut allergy would mean. She'd be assigned to a special table where she'd eat her lunch alone each day, and a special "No Peanuts" sign would hang from the door of any classroom she stepped inside, like a modern-day scarlet letter. I hoped she wouldn't be bullied the way I had been.

Jeff reached over and squeezed my hand, "It's going to be okay," he said. "We'll figure it out." His forced optimism fell flat on my ears. He searched the radio for a song that might help lift both our moods and tuned to the local country station, which was playing "Country Roads," our favorite song and the anthem played at every West Virginia football game. John Denver's voice, both strong and sweet, came through the car speakers. I let myself be carried back to the WVU parking lot, where we had shared bags of greasy potato chips, pepperoni rolls, and cold beers with Tom and Sam. I tried to lean into the chorus and focus on the happier days, but all I could feel was the darkness instead of the stars.

You're being ridiculous, I thought to myself. *It's a peanut allergy, not a death sentence. There are so many things that could be worse.* Tom had navigated his diabetes diagnosis with courage, never letting it keep him from doing what he wanted, like mountain biking or white-water rafting. *Be more like Tom,* I thought, *be brave.* I tried to focus on John Denver, but the song stopped abruptly. Jeff and I looked at each other, confused.

"Pardon the interruption," the DJ's voice shifted seriously. "This just in: another fatal shooting has taken place in Northwest, D.C. The victim, a seventy-two-year-old man, Pascal Charlot, was attacked while walking down Georgia Avenue. This brings the death count to five, including twenty-five-year-old Lori Anne Lewis-Rivera, who was shot and killed this afternoon while vacuuming her minivan at a gas station in Kensington, MD. Police and first responders are currently working across state lines to share information."

I caught Jeff's reaction as his eyes grew wide. "Let's hurry up and get home," he said somberly. "I'm ready for this day to be over." I checked the rearview mirror to see Emma sleeping peacefully, unaware of how her world had just changed.

Jeff activated the garage door as we pulled onto the driveway, both of us thankful to have made it home safely. I

Chapter Five: Peanuts

crawled into the backseat of the car to unsnap Emma's buckle and lifted her carefully out of her seat. She stayed asleep as we walked upstairs to her bedroom. I changed her into her pajamas and tossed her red and black outfit onto the floor.

From downstairs, I could hear Jeff going through the mail and playing the audio messages on the answering machine. A loud, "BEEP," sounding before and after each one.

"You have ten messages," the machine sounded robotically as it played the first message.

"Hi, Cara and Jeff. Oh, my goodness! I hope Emma is okay!" came Sheku's worried voice. "I'm making that saffron rice you love for dinner. Call me when you get home, no matter how late, and I'll bring it over. I'm here if you need anything!" The answering machine moved onto the next message.

"Hey guys! It's Tom. Just calling to make sure you guys are safe. Those shootings in D.C. are crazy! It made national news. Anyway, call me when you get a chance."

Emma slept in my arms as I stood in the doorway of her bedroom, listening intently as each message played.

"Cara, it's Susan. Thank you again for calling from the doctor's office earlier. I'm so sorry I gave her those M&Ms right before her nap. I feel like this is all my fault. I know you said you're staying home with her tomorrow, but I'd love to come over and visit if that's okay."

It wasn't Susan's fault—it was mine. I'd bought those stupid M&M's, not her. How could I trust anything she ate from now on? The answering machine rolled on.

"Hi, sweetie, it's Mom. I know you've had a rough day, but Dad and I are ready to jump in the car tomorrow and come help you if you need us. Also, the national news is reporting several shootings in your area. What is going on? We're worried sick about you all. Just call us and let us know, okay? We love you."

Each message made me feel everything again, all at once, which was the opposite of what I wanted. I didn't want to feel anything else tonight. Worse yet, Jeff had to catch an early flight to Port Charles, Louisiana, for work. I'd be alone.

Chapter Six

Warmth

"Hey, honey, it's Sharon." The last message on the machine played out loud. "I was just calling to check on you. I know you must be scared right now, but don't be afraid. It's going to be okay! I promise! You are strong!" She continued, "I hope you don't mind, but Rob gathered several of us after school. He told us about Emma, and we prayed for your family. I just wanted to let you know that we are here for you. Love you, friend!"

My eyes grew wide. They had gathered to pray for us, even after I'd coldly rejected her that morning? Why would they do that? These people weren't my family, and yet they were treating us like we were. I thought about the words from Sharon's desk calendar that morning and imagined them stopping everything they were doing to gather and pray for my family, for Emma. *Fear not, don't be afraid.*

The tears I'd been holding back all day started to well up in my eyes, and an unfamiliar *warmth* started to spread through my hands.

Jeff poked his head into the room, interrupting my thoughts. "You okay?" he whispered, not wanting to wake Emma up. I was thankful that the room was dark enough to conceal my tears.

"Yeah, I'm ok," I said quietly. "Go pack for your flight."

He tried to convince me to sleep in shifts, but I wouldn't hear of it. I'd taken the day off from school anyway. Why should we both be exhausted? He kissed us both on the head and went reluctantly to bed. I tucked Emma's blanket around her and let my hand settle over her chest so I could check her breathing.

Her clothes from the day lay in a pile on the floor. When I'd dressed her that morning, everything had been different— she'd been healthy. Now, we'd have to think about everything she ate, forever. And if we got it wrong, it could kill her. A wave of anger pushed the *warmth* of my friend's prayers away, and without thinking, I marched across the room, balled up her clothes and threw them into the trash, knocking the can over in the process. *Good*, I thought. *Throw it all away.* Emma stirred in her bed but didn't wake up. I settled into the rocking chair across from her bed, mentally preparing myself for the long night ahead.

The minutes and hours dragged on. I kept replaying the events of the day over in my head: teachers running in the hallway, the verses from Sharon's desk, the shootings, and Emma's swollen eyes. I tried to push the thoughts away, but they were quickly replaced with the faces of the five innocent people who had been gunned down. Did they have children, husbands, or wives? Were their loved ones sitting somewhere in a dark room tonight, too?

Pull it together, I thought. Maybe I could borrow something from Rob and Sharon's playbook. I tried to remember the Bible verses from Sharon's desk again. What did they say? *Fear not, do not be afraid?* I wished I'd memorized them.

Fear not, don't be afraid, fear not, don't be afraid. I repeated the parts of the verses I could remember over and over again until slowly, without realizing, I did the one thing I wasn't supposed to do: I fell asleep.

Chapter Seven

Fear Not

"Mommy!" Emma's voice woke me from my sleep.

I jolted upright. The rocking chair lurched forward violently, and I had to lift my arm to shield my eyes from the sunlight pouring through the window.

"Mommy, I hungry," she demanded.

My mind felt like a rock tumbler, sorting and churning each event from the day before. I stood up too quickly and had to grab the corner of her white dresser for support.

"Mommy! Waffles?"

Waffles? Were waffles safe for her to eat? What about her favorite yogurt or toast, or anything? How was I supposed to know what was safe and what was not? My heart beat faster.

Her eyes were still a bit swollen, and her appetite had returned just as the doctor had predicted last night. My hand felt clammy against the dresser.

"Mommy! Let's go eat!" She jumped out of bed and came running at me, full speed, knocking me sideways. "Let's go! Let's go! Let's gooooo EAT!" she jumped up and down. The tremor in my hand returned.

WHOOSH! I tugged at my ears, trying to clear the sound. I could see Emma standing in front of me with her arms up, but I couldn't make myself move. An invisible magnet seemed to be pulling everything in the room sideways. I needed Jeff. Where was he? Then I remembered, he was probably halfway to the airport.

"Mommmmmmmy! Waffles!" she wailed, waving her arms in little violent circles as I fought my lungs to cooperate. I grabbed her hand for support.

"Mommy! PLEEEEASSSEEE!" I gasped for air, trying to take deep breaths, but my lungs wouldn't cooperate.

"Brinnnnng," the bedroom telephone sounded. *Oh, thank you! Maybe it's Jeff,* I thought, *please let it be Jeff.* I maneuvered us both to my bedroom, Emma crying hysterically now, as I grabbed for the phone.

"Hello? Jeff?"

"Cara? No, it's Sheku." She could hear the panic in my voice. "Is something wrong?"

"Sheku!" I cried, unable to catch my breath.

"I'm coming over," she said without hesitating. "I'll use my key."

I used the wall as an anchor and slid myself down onto the floor, gripping the edges of the carpet between my shaking fingers. *WHOOSH, WHOOSH, WHOOSH!*

The sound of Sheku's name made Emma stop crying, and she plopped down next to me with concerned eyes. "Sheku?" she asked innocently. I couldn't catch my breath to answer her.

I heard the front door open as Sheku called out, "Cara! Where are you?" Thankfully, Emma answered for us both.

"Shekuww! Shekuww! Shekuww!" She stood up and ran to the steep landing at the top of the steps.

Chapter Seven: Fear Not

"There you are, my sweet girl!" she said, taking the steps two at a time so she could reach her before Emma attempted the stairs on her own.

She swooped her up and ran down the hallway towards me, kneeling to grab my hands.

"Cara, what's going on? Do I need to call 911?"

"No, don't!" I begged. "Don't scare Emma!"

"Then I'm going to need to see you slow down your breathing," she said firmly.

If I ever needed God's help, this was it. I leaned on the Bible verses from Sharon's desk calendar.

Fear not, don't be afraid, fear not, don't be afraid, I thought, developing a cadence that matched my breath. Breathe in, breathe out, fear not, don't be afraid.

"Yes," said Sheku. "Breathe in and out, in and out."

I did this repeatedly until, mercifully, the pinwheel in my brain began to slow down. The room began to come back into focus, and I unclenched the edges of the carpet.

Sheku held my hands tightly and looked me gently in the eyes. "You're safe now."

I took another deep breath, but my head felt thick, foggy, and jumbled. "Am I?" I asked. Emma sat nearby, wide-eyed and taking it all in. I suddenly felt ashamed.

"Yes, you are," she said again. "I think you must have had a panic attack." She hugged me tightly. "It's going to be okay, I promise."

"Mommy? Hungry?" came Emma's voice.

"Emma, darling, do you want to go watch Barney? How about some rice that I made?" Emma jumped up and grabbed Sheku's hand, but glanced backwards over her shoulder at me.

I felt like a failure. I crawled into my bed, pulled the covers tightly over my head, and curled into a ball. I wanted to sleep until the world I woke up to finally made sense again. Where there were no snipers, or Epi-Pens, or tremors in my hands. I closed my eyes and fell into a fitful sleep.

But while I slept, in those lost hours where I tossed and turned, fighting a battle with demons of my own making, another innocent person, Caroline Seawall, was shot and wounded as she loaded Halloween decorations into her minivan.

Chapter Eight

The Prayer

The white wooden shutters in our bedroom were no match for the sunlight on Monday morning. It pierced through the darkness just as I hit the alarm clock, which was blasting, "Times Like These," by The Foo Fighters. It took everything in my power to open my eyes, since I'd spent most of the weekend sleeping and worrying that I might have another panic attack.

Jeff, back from his trip, tried to distract and encourage me. "How about we rent a movie?" he suggested. "Let's take your mind off everything. Nothing good is going to happen if you stay in bed." But I just wanted to be left alone. Thankfully, Sheku brought us dinner, so I didn't need to cook.

The neighborhood had been eerily quiet all weekend because no one felt safe going outside. Everyone who lived in the DMV was on high alert. The hunt for the sniper consumed both the news cycle and all our thoughts. The FBI, Department of Defense, and every police officer in D.C., Maryland, and Virginia were working furiously to locate a suspect. But so far, all they had were empty bullet casings and lots of false leads.

"Only go outside if absolutely necessary," was the directive from the authorities. "If you must go outside, don't walk in a straight line. Weave, make sharp turns, and stay low to the ground." And as I drove Emma to Susan's house that morning, that was my plan: weave, make sharp turns and stay low to the ground. I'd set my alarm early that morning, hoping to get to school before everyone else so I could gather my thoughts and get my classroom ready in peace.

But my hands still shook slightly as I unsnapped her from her car seat, propped her on my hip, and ran as fast as I could up to the front porch. I gave Susan Emma's new medical pouch, complete with two newly prescribed EpiPens, Benadryl, and her health insurance card. We'd agreed on "safe" foods for Emma to eat from now on, and I was thankful for Susan's willingness to still babysit with this new responsibility. I gave Emma one last hug and ran back to my car, ducking and trying to make myself small. *Fear not, don't be afraid*, I told myself.

As I made the turn out of the neighborhood and headed to school, I replayed the conversation I'd had with Sheku over the weekend.

"Just take one day at a time," she said softly. "You'll figure it all out as you go. You just need to retrain your monkey brain."

"My what?" I'd asked.

"Monkey brain," she said kindly. "Right now, your thoughts are out of control, like a monkey in a cage, bouncing off the walls. But if you give a monkey a task or something to play with, it instantly settles down. Why don't you try listening to some music?" I thought about how I always had music running through my head anyway. Maybe I could use that habit to stop another panic attack.

"Is that what you do?" I asked. "I doubt you've ever had to retrain your brain, though. You're so strong."

Chapter Eight: The Prayer

She paused, looking at me compassionately. "Oh, Cara. If you only knew," she said. "I fight my own battles every day, too. We all do. Try distracting yourself with music for now."

I switched from one radio station to the next, searching for a song that might do the trick, but a disc jockey interrupted my search with a special announcement. Before he spoke, I knew what was coming.

"Pardon the interruption, we have breaking news. A thirteen-year-old has just been shot outside of Benjamin Tasker Middle School in Bowie, Maryland. Police have swarmed the area and are searching for suspects or clues. A white van was reported leaving the area at the time of the shooting, but no other information is available at this time." A child? I must have heard that wrong. A child? Please God, not a child.

I pulled into the school's empty parking lot as the news coverage continued. I desperately wanted to stay in my car and listen, but I was terrified of being outside and exposed, especially since the sniper seemed to now be targeting schools. I grabbed my teacher bag, took a deep breath, and put my hand on the door handle, but then I froze. I couldn't bring myself to open the door.

Out of the corner of my eye, I saw another car pulling into the parking lot, it was Sharon. She pulled into her spot a few spaces away. I watched as she slowly gathered her things from the front seat, opened her car door, and casually strolled through the parking lot. There was no sense of urgency in her walk, no zigzagging or dodging. She even seemed to be smiling.

She reached the front entrance of the school, turned around, and saw me sitting like a statue in the front seat of my car. A smile stretched across her face as she held the door open for me, motioning for me to come inside. I was dumbfounded. I could barely bring myself to open the door of my car, and there she stood, brave and unafraid. What was she thinking?

Her smile gave me the courage I needed, so I took a deep breath, pulled the handle, and ran as fast as I could to the front door.

"Well, now," she grinned. "You move pretty quick when you need to!"

"I didn't think I had a choice," I said quietly.

"Honey, you always have a choice," she replied, gently giving my arm a squeeze as I steadied myself. We collected our bags and headed down the empty hallway to our rooms. The school was quiet; we were the first ones there.

"How's Emma doing?" she asked.

"She's fine," I lied, trying to sound composed, but even I could hear the falseness of my words. "She's too young to understand what a peanut allergy means anyway."

Sharon stopped walking and turned to look at me. I stopped walking, too. "It's going to be okay. I promise. God has it all under control."

There it was again. God. She spoke about God like He was her best friend. Like she knew everything about Him and all of it was good. It made me long for the God of my childhood. I couldn't fake feeling brave for one more second.

"But how do you know that?" I demanded, my voice a little sharper than I intended. "How can you know that? One trace of the wrong food and Emma could die! I can't protect her from that. And now we have snipers hunting us, hunting children for God's sake. You walked through the parking lot like none of that even existed! Aren't you afraid?"

She paused. I could see her choosing her next words carefully. "Honey, of course I'm afraid. But I can't let that change the way I live."

I shook my head. "I don't understand. How do you keep it all together?"

Chapter Eight: The Prayer

"Cara, on my own, I can't. Just ask my family." She smiled playfully, then continued. "But since I've discovered a deeper relationship with Jesus, I've come to realize I don't have to! I can walk through anything this life has for me by surrendering my life into Jesus' hands. I'm so grateful I have a Savior." She fixed her eyes on mine. "Cara, the way you love Emma, the way you want to protect her, the way you delight in everything she does, and the way you hurt when she hurts, that's exactly how Jesus feels about you."

Sharon's words sank in. Jesus loved me the same way I loved Emma?

"How is that possible?" I asked. "I don't even know Him."

Sharon's shoulders softened, she paused, took a deep breath, and asked me the same question she'd asked in that hallway just a week earlier. "Cara, do you want to pray with me?" She extended her open hands to me as her words hung in the air. The images of my childhood bullies swirled around my head, but this felt safe. Sharon felt safe. And I desperately needed hope.

"Okay," I whispered, letting her hands wrap around mine. She closed her eyes and bowed her head. So did I.

And then she prayed.

"Father God, thank you that you have moved in my life and are helping me to grow in your love, teaching me more and more each day. And thank you for the friendship you have allowed between Cara and me that has led to this moment. I know it is through your power, not mine. But, right now, God, your beloved daughter Cara is scared, and I know that is not the way you intended her to live. Father, cover Cara with the peace that surpasses all understanding so that she can live a life of joy, walking with you and your son Jesus. Open her heart to experience your glory and receive the gift of your grace. Open her eyes to see the beauty and blessings around her. And Father, wrap your loving arms around her so she knows exactly who you are. In Jesus' precious name, Amen."

As Sharon spoke those words in that empty hallway, the ceiling and floor seemed to drift away. We stood, heads bowed, hands locked, lifting our hearts to God in prayer. The same *warmth* I'd felt in Emma's bedroom returned, but this time, it spread past my fingers and into my heart. I wanted to stay in that hallway forever.

After what felt like forever, we both opened our eyes. Mine were wet with tears. Sharon squeezed my hands tightly and smiled radiantly. Overcome and bewildered, I blurted out the only sentence I could muster.

"Sharon, what was that?!"

Sharon laughed, gave me a mama bear hug, and said, "Oh, honey, that was JESUS!"

Chapter Nine

A Mustard Seed

But our hallway prayer didn't stop the shootings. On Wednesday, October 9, Dean Myer, a Vietnam veteran, was gunned down at a Sunoco station in Manassas, Virginia. Two days later, Kenneth Bridges, a businessman from Philadelphia, was shot at an Exxon station in Fredericksburg. Then, late Monday night, Linda Franklin, an FBI agent, was gunned down at her local Home Depot station as she simply shopped for her family. We were living in a war zone but fighting an invisible enemy. The death toll stood at ten, and 13-year-old Iran Brown, the boy who had been shot outside his middle school, lay in a hospital bed fighting for his life.

And somehow, in the middle of this hell, I'd found peace in the hallway of an elementary school.

I'd spent the rest of the school day trying to understand what had happened in that hallway. Because if, like Sharon said, that feeling had really been Jesus, pursuing it would mean taking the well-laid puzzle pieces of my life and sending them crashing onto the floor. What would my friends from synagogue say? And what about my parents? How could a Jew like me also love Jesus? That thought was more terrifying to me than snipers or peanuts.

So, when I got home from school that night, I didn't say anything to Jeff about the prayer. It all felt like Pandora's box. Once I opened it, there was no going back. So I stayed silent.

The next morning, before Emma and I left for school, Jeff hugged us both more tightly than usual. The entire community had been rocked by Iran Brown's shooting, including Maryland Chief of Police, Charles Moose. Chief Moose had become the face of the Beltway Sniper investigation, and we all tuned in nightly for his updates on the case. He was stoic, strong, and authoritative. But as Chief Moose stood at the press podium, delivering the details of the shooting of an innocent child, he looked defeated. The sniper had left a tarot death card with the hand-written words, "Call me God," in the woods near the shooting, seemingly taunting Chief Moose for telling the press days earlier that, "Your children are safe." Tears of rage ran openly down his face as he gripped the sides of the podium, vowing that they would leave no stone unturned until they hunted down the coward who would target innocent children.

Many of the local school districts considered closing schools, but ultimately decided to remain open with new safety regulations in place. Window shades would remain shut to prevent the sniper from getting a clear shot into a classroom full of children, and outside activities, including sporting events and recess, were canceled until further notice.

"Be careful out there today," Jeff said quietly.

"You, too," I answered. "Head straight home. No stopping for gas, okay?" We hugged one more time and headed out.

I started the car, pulled out of the driveway, and headed towards Susan's house. I checked my rearview mirror to see Emma's curly hair poking out from around the edges of her Gymboree hat. I wished I could tell her about what had happened in the hallway. I wanted her and Jeff to experience that feeling, too. I just didn't know how that could be possible. Saying yes to Jesus would change everything for me.

The October trees were just beginning to turn colors, and wet leaves stuck to the road, leaving a trail for me to follow all the way into Susan's neighborhood. A light rain fell, and my windshield wipers created a soothing rhythm so I could focus on what came next: getting Emma safely into Susan's house. But this time, I had a plan.

"Emma, ready to play kangaroo?" I asked as I pulled into Susan's driveway, trying my best to sound upbeat and calm. I reached back and unbuckled the straps on her car seat.

"Yes, Mommy!" she clapped and wiggled herself from the back seat to the front, onto my lap. We'd practiced before we'd left this morning, and Emma knew exactly what to do, even if she didn't understand why we were doing it. I unzipped my jacket to make space for her body as she snuggled deeply into my chest.

Fear not, don't be afraid, I repeated to myself.

"Ready, Mommy!" she said loudly as she squeezed her arms around my torso.

I scanned the surrounding woods that backed to Susan's yard for any movement before slowly putting my hand on the door handle, counting down out loud so Emma could be ready.

"Ready? Here we go, 3, 2 … 1!"

But suddenly, a tree branch off to my right snapped as a squirrel jumped and then scurried across the driveway right in front of the car. I jolted violently, turning both our bodies away from the car window. My heart began to race and I froze. Emma let out a giggle, thinking the game had begun.

WHOOSH!

"Mommy, GOOOOO!" she squealed.

The dreaded *whoosh* sound grew louder, and my heart began to pound. Emma's demands for me to move became shriller. I knew what was about to happen. My hands began to tremble.

"Not now! Oh God, not now!" I looked around the car for anything that might ground me. But as the word *God* came out of my mouth, something clicked in my head, and without warning, the words on Sharon's desk calendar came tumbling out of my mouth as a plea.

"Do not fear, I am with you! Don't be afraid! I will help you!"

The words surprised me. I knew my prayer wasn't perfect, but I hoped it was close enough. Emma stopped squirming and peaked up at me from between the warm layers of my coat.

"Mommy, what?" she asked sweetly. I took a moment to think about how to answer her and finally decided on the only answer I had.

"That was a prayer to God," I said, looking down at her. She smiled back at me, satisfied, then snuggled back into my jacket. I exhaled deeply and repeated the prayer silently again to myself, giving my "monkey brain" something else to focus on. I could feel my breath slow down and my body relax.

Did I do that or did God? I thought. Either way, I was grateful. I opened the car door, held her tightly, and zigzagged us to Susan's house. I handed Susan Emma's Epi-Pen bag and gave her an extra hug before turning to leave.

I ran back to my car, thinking more about dodging raindrops than bullets, and headed to school, my heart feeling less heavy than it had in months. "Thank you, God," I said out loud. I couldn't help but smile at my newfound favorite word: *God*. I'd always known God, but this felt different, more intimate, like a loving father and child, just as Sharon had said. Everything in my heart wanted to know Him more.

Chapter Nine: A Mustard Seed

I tested it out again in the silence of the car. "Thank you, GOD," I said, and then laughed out loud as I imagined my car as a "holy rolling" mobile, now anointed with prayer. I couldn't remember ever speaking to God like this before. I'd felt His presence as a child, but I'd never spoken to Him like this before.

And as I turned onto the main road towards school, a new name unexpectedly welled up inside me.

Jesus.

Jesus: a name I wasn't sure I'd ever spoken in my life. It stood like a domino at the start of a very long chain reaction and got stuck in my throat. A mixture of guilt and confusion clouded my moment of joy. After everything my people had suffered at the hands of Christians, pursuing Jesus seemed like a deep betrayal.

Memories of singing melodic Hebrew songs like "Shalom Rav" and "Oseh Shalom," songs of peace, at Jewish sleep-away camp with my friends, our hands linked as the sun set, reminded me of the peace of Sharon's hallway prayer. Why did these two beautiful things have to be separate? Weren't they born of the same thing, the same love? Why couldn't they coexist if both brought such peace to me? It felt like a spiritual tug-of-war.

As I made the final turn into the school parking lot, I realized there was only one person I could trust with my questions. I needed to see Sharon.

But the moment I stepped into the building, everything felt heavy. The usual hustle of teachers making copies or laughing in hallways was missing. Groups of teachers stood huddled in the hallway, heads down, speaking in hushed tones.

"This feels like 9/11 all over again," said one. "We can't keep the kids inside forever, they'll go crazy!"

"Do you think we still have to go outside for bus duty?" I heard another ask tentatively.

"I guess so. If we don't protect them, who will? But you better believe I'll be praying the whole time."

This last part caught my attention. I wanted to turn and join the huddle, to ask if I could pray too, to ask a million questions. I knew there were other Christians at my school, but what did they believe?

But my fear won out. "Good morning," I said, and continued my usual detour through the teacher's lounge to drop off my lunchbox.

The teacher's lounge was empty and quiet. The shades over the windows were closed, and yet, somehow, the inside of this room still looked beautiful. Streaks of light fell softly over everything, the sun unaware and unbothered by the shootings outside. I wondered if God was unbothered, too. If He really was in control, why wasn't He controlling all of this chaos?

I opened the refrigerator to play my usual game of lunchbox Jenga, maneuvering other people's lunches so I could squeeze mine in, when a loud, chipper voice pierced the air.

"Morning, Cara!" I jumped backwards and let out a yelp. I turned to see Rob, looking sheepish, his arms extended in apology.

"So sorry, Cara! I didn't mean to scare you!"

I gathered myself and smiled, "Morning, Rob. It's okay," I said. Startled as I was, who could be mad at this man?

"How are you doing this morning?" he asked genuinely. But I caught something behind his eyes that made me pause. In a matter of seconds, pieces started coming together in my head. Sharon and Rob were friends. Close friends. Had Sharon told him about the prayer?

Chapter Nine: A Mustard Seed

"I'm fine," I said, turning back to the open fridge to avoid his eyes. I wondered what he might say if he knew that I had just recited a Bible verse from a Christian desk calendar on my way to school.

"Ok, good. Stop by if you ever need anything. My door is always open," he said, turning and heading down the hallway to his office, leaving me alone in the teacher's lounge. I stared blankly into the crowded refrigerator full of pats of orphaned butter, weeks-old yogurts, and unnamed spills. The answers I needed were not going to be found there. Maybe the person I needed to speak with this morning wasn't Sharon; maybe it was Rob. I closed the refrigerator door and felt myself being pulled like a magnet to Rob's office. As promised, the door was open.

I knocked tentatively. Rob looked up from what he was doing and smiled widely, "Hey again!" he said cheerfully.

"Hey," I said hesitantly. "I'm sorry to bother you before school."

"You're no bother, Cara," he said cheerfully. "We're both early this morning, come on in. Just give me a sec to wrap up this email."

I stepped inside, placed my teacher bag on the floor, and took a seat in one of the chairs he'd carefully placed in front of his desk. As he worked, I let my eyes wander around the room. Pictures of his wife, Charlene, and their three children sat on the corner of the desk. His bookshelf was full of educational material, children's literature, and trinkets. I'd seen them hundreds of times, but this morning, something else on his desk caught my eye. It was a small photo album, propped open on a tiny metal stand. But rather than photos of people, someone had handwritten Bible verses on colored craft paper and placed a different one in each sleeve. I leaned forward to see the verse for the day: "Be still, and know that I am God;" (Psalm 46:10 NIV)

Rob hit the last stroke on his keyboard dramatically and proclaimed loudly, "Done!" as he swiveled in his chair to look at me. "What can I do for you this morning?" he asked.

He seemed unfazed by all the new safety regulations and the terror that lay just outside his window. I took a deep breath and pointed to the verse on his desk.

"I like your photo album," I said meekly. A knowing smile spread across his face, confirming my suspicion that he had, indeed, spoken to Sharon. He reached for it and the verse on the page.

"Thanks! This was a gift to me from a dear friend. She took some of my favorite verses and put this together for me for my birthday!" He turned it around so that he could see the verse I had just read. "Be still and know that I am God," he smiled as he read the verse out loud. "That's a favorite of mine. Do you know it?"

I shook my head, no. I paused, trying to give myself time to think. He sat patiently, a warm smile offering the space I needed. Hundreds of tiny details about the way he treated his staff, the parents, and, more importantly, the children at this school gave me the courage I needed to ask the next question.

"What does it mean?"

His shoulders softened as he leaned back into his chair. He seemed to understand the importance of his response, and he took his time with his words. And, like a seasoned teacher, he turned the question back to me. "What do you think it means?"

"I'm honestly not sure," I answered.

"Ok, then. How does it make you feel?" Bingo. He could see by the look on my face that he'd struck a chord.

How could I explain to Rob that the one thing that was giving me peace was the very thing that had tormented me as a child on a school bus and done unimaginable harm to my people? How could I even speak the name, *Jesus*, out loud?

"I feel like God wants me to know Him more, but I don't know how to find Him," I said, avoiding using the name *Jesus*.

"Well, it sounds like you're both searching for each other. What a wonderful game of hide and seek. I wonder who will win?" He smiled kindly.

I laughed quietly. "Well, lately I've gotten pretty good at running in zigzag lines so it might be hard for Him to find me," I winced, thinking of my game of kangaroo with Emma this morning.

"Impossible, Cara," he said firmly, his voice becoming bolder as he straightened up in his chair. "God knows every hair on your head because He created you! A little zigging and zagging can't throw Him off. And that verse, 'Be Still and Know that I am God,' is His invitation for you to run towards Him. But to find Him, you're going to have to create space in your heart first. Quiet your mind and surrender everything into His hands. Everything else will simply fade away."

"Everything?" I asked, wondering how much prayer might be needed to eradicate peanuts, catch a sniper, and tell my family everything.

"Yes, everything. The evil you see every day is the result of our collective choices. That won't change. But when we pray, we get to step into God's presence where we are renewed, restored, and reminded that Jesus' love is bigger than the evil that exists in our world. That's how I wake up every day with hope in my heart, even in the middle of sniper attacks."

He shifted his weight, swiveled his chair, and stood up. He reached into his pocket and extended his hand, opening his palm to reveal a small cross. "I keep this cross in my pocket as a reminder of that hope."

My eyes grew wide as I stared at the cross in his hands.

It was a symbol that had always been shrouded in mystery to me. As a child, I'd always felt terrified by the images of Jesus, hanging on that cross, blood dripping from his hands and feet as the crown of thorns tore into his flesh. I would always look away, frightened by the image of what man was capable of doing to his fellow man.

A memory resurfaced of my best friend preparing for her First Holy Communion when we were just children. She had shown me the delicate white satin dress with matching veil she got to wear the day she said "Yes" to Jesus. I remembered feeling jealous that she'd get to wear something so beautiful.

"We are all born sinners, so we need Jesus to save us," she had said, repeating the sentence she'd learned in church. Was that the meaning of original sin? That it lived inside all of us, including me?

Rob spoke again, "We couldn't rescue ourselves, so God sent His son, Jesus, to rescue us instead. The cross is a reminder of that sacrifice because Jesus loves you that much. It's an invitation to life, not a condemnation. And if you want to understand that love more, ask God to help you. I promise you, time with Him will be the most wonderful thing you can imagine. Just make room for Him and be still." I thought about the hallway prayer.

I stared at the cross again. But instead of feeling afraid, I felt something else. I felt sorrow for what had happened to Jesus at the hands of man. Jesus had suffered horrifically at the hands of people just like me.

Rob put the cross gently back into his pocket. "I think you and Jesus have a lot to talk about."

"I think we do too," I said, just as the morning school bell rang and hundreds of children began to fill the hallway.

Chapter Ten

Gifts

The saying, "Gossip spreads like wildfire," must have found its origin inside a teacher's lounge because within days of my conversations with Rob and Sharon, other Christians at Algonkian Elementary got wind that Jesus was chasing after me. I worried that too many people knew, but it was hard to deny the way I was feeling. And each morning, as I got to my desk, someone secretly started leaving me gifts to let me know that Jesus did indeed love me, even if I still hadn't said his name out loud.

The first morning, there was a single red rose with the words, "Jesus loves You" written on a note card. The second morning, there was a beautifully framed 5x7 picture of the first verse I'd read from Sharon's calendar: Isaiah 41:10, "Fear Not, for I am with you," a verse that I now had memorized. I made the bold decision to display the picture framed verse on my desk.

Each morning, I stood staring at the evidence of undeserved love that my coworkers and God were lavishing upon me. I hadn't heard the *whoosh* or felt the tremor in my hand for days.

I went to Sharon's room on the first morning to give her

a hug and thank her for the rose, only to be met by a confused look on her face.

"Honey, that wasn't me," she said wide-eyed.

"Do you think it was Rob?" I asked.

"He's not even here today," she said.

"Then who was it?" I demanded.

Sharon smiled sheepishly, "I miiiiight have told a few people about what was happening," she tilted her head innocently, "only so that they could pray for you, that's all! It's the same group of ladies who prayed for you when Emma had her allergic reaction. Most of us worship together on Sunday mornings at Riverside Church. They love you." I should've felt upset at her for the breach of confidence, but instead, it made me immensely happy.

But on the third morning, my secret gift-giver left me something that brought me to a crossroad. When I arrived at my classroom that morning, I could see there was something on my desk before I even turned the lights on. As I got closer to see what it was, I realized it was a small, wooden cross keychain. It probably weighed less than an ounce, but it weighed heavily on my mind. Owning my own cross felt like a step too far. It was the first concrete evidence of what I was doing. I knew I couldn't continue this way, secretly exploring Jesus without telling Jeff or my family.

My classroom was still empty, giving me time to think. I stared at the cross, lying right next to the Isaiah 41:10 verse. The two things seemed so disconnected, so separated by the experiences that were attached to each one. The verse was given to me by teachers who cared for me, and the other brought me right back to the judgment of my childhood bullies. I tried to work out which one had been misrepresented. Was it Jesus I was afraid of, or the people who tried to speak for Him?

I thought about the words from Rob's office. He'd said

Chapter Ten: Gifts

that if I made space, Jesus would find me. I desperately wished he would. Was he to be feared, or loved? I had to know. I closed my eyes and hoped I could pray like Sharon had.

"God?" My words broke the silence of my dark classroom. I opened one eye to make sure I was still alone. I was. I began again. "God? I've been afraid of so much for so long. I don't want to be afraid anymore. Help me understand who you really are," I filled my lungs with as much air as I could, held it, and then slowly let it all go.

Images of each child who had shamed me came into sharp focus, exactly as I remembered them from my childhood. It all felt so heavy, too heavy. I'd been carrying it around for so long that it had attached itself to my soul. And I didn't want to carry it anymore. I thought about the kindness I felt now from the Christians at this school.

Maybe to really understand who Jesus was, I needed to forgive first. This hurt couldn't exist in my heart if I wanted to make room for something new to grow. They were just kids, flawed and broken, just like me. Maybe we all needed a hallway prayer.

I took another deep breath and exhaled it all. "I forgive you," I whispered into the silence of the room.

I opened my eyes and stared at the keychain cross. I picked it up and placed it in the palm of my hand. It didn't frighten me anymore. "Okay," I said out loud, "I guess it's time I met you for myself." I reached for a tissue, wrapped the cross gently inside, and tucked it into my bag just as my fifth graders walked into the room.

I stepped away from my desk to greet each of them. "Morning, you all!" I said cheerfully, reminding myself that it was my job to make them feel safe today.

"My parents almost wouldn't let me come today," said one. "They think it's crazy we still have school after that kid got shot."

"I know," responded another. "My mom won't let me get on the bus or go outside at all. She's driving me and my sister to school every day." A worried buzzing of conversation between each of them spread around the room. They were all afraid, but just like 9/11, we had been told not to talk with them about anything but school today.

"It's okay," I said confidently. "I've got some great things lined up for us to do inside today. You'll see, it will be fun!" But I wasn't sure they were convinced.

They finished unpacking their backpacks and settled into their seats for the start of the day. As I took my seat at the front of the room, I wondered how Sharon's students were doing.

Soon, Rob's voice boomed across the intercom with his usual, "Goooooood mooooorning Algonkian Bobcats! As we begin another day, let us pause for a moment of silence." I looked at the faces of my worried students and decided that if I wasn't allowed to talk to them about what was happening, I could at least share what was giving me peace. I closed my eyes, bowed my head, and prayed silently. *Dear God, help me to be brave so I can be the teacher these kids need today. Help me to push away fear and to be still in your presence instead.* I could sense twenty-six pairs of eyes on me, wondering and watching, but I continued for the full minute until Rob broke the silence. When I finally opened my eyes, I realized that several of my students had bowed their heads, too. We shared a smile. I took a deep breath and knew what I needed to do when I got home: it was time to tell Jeff.

I tried to focus on the history lesson I was teaching my students that afternoon, but I was quietly rehearsing the biggest conversation of my life. There would be no turning back.

I picked Emma up after school and, to her delight, played another round of kangaroo from Susan's house to our car. She

Chapter Ten: Gifts

sang along with the Disney CD I'd popped into the player, giving me more time to think as we made our drive back home.

I pulled into the garage, unsnapped Emma from her car seat, and walked into the kitchen to find the answering machine blinking. Tom had left a message. "Hey guys, just checking in on everyone. Just hope you are all safe. Give me a call back when you get a chance." I made a mental note to call him later.

My parents had also left a worried message, but for the first time ever, I hesitated to dial their number. I'd always been a horrible liar, and the truth was, now I had a secret. Emma, ever my little shadow, held my hand as I dialed her Baba and Nana's number.

"Hi Mom, hi Dad," I said as cheerfully as I could.

"Hi, sweetie," came their voices. "How's everyone doing? We're worried sick about all of you." I adored them so much, and the last thing I wanted was for them to worry, so I told them the truth.

"Actually, we're doing better than you'd think," I said, thinking of the prayer in my classroom. Then I changed the subject quickly with my best weapon, their granddaughter. "Want to talk to Emma?" I asked, already knowing their answer.

Emma loved chatting away to them with her ever-growing vocabulary, and they loved soaking it all in, a win-win for me. I handed her the cordless phone and watched as she scurried off to the other room for "pwifacy." She could talk with them for hours on her own if I let her. I grabbed the ironing board and a pile of wrinkled clothes from the laundry basket, turned on the television, wondering when Chief Moose might have another update.

I carefully folded a pant leg, sprayed it lightly with starch, and watched with satisfaction as steam rose from the fabric and a neat crease emerged. I flipped the pants over. Fold, spray, steam, repeat, fold, spray, steam, repeat; a repetitive and soothing rhythm for my monkey brain.

Suddenly, a melody playing on the T.V. screen interrupted my routine. When I looked up, I saw a massive auditorium filled with thousands of people, all singing one of the most beautiful songs I'd ever heard. And they were singing to Jesus.

An announcer broke in. "WOW Worship, a compilation of today's top Christian hits, will inspire and encourage you as you worship." I stood frozen, the hot iron still in my hand, releasing its steam into the air.

People of all ages, races, and backgrounds stood together, singing. A caption flashed across the screen with the title of the song: "Shout to the Lord" by Darlene Zschech. I'd never seen anything like it: people with their eyes closed, hands raised to the sky, completely surrendered. Was this what Sharon meant when she talked about "worshipping" in church? I thought of my home synagogue, standing as a congregation reciting prayer. I had one powerful thought: *Please let heaven feel just like this song.*

And then, just as suddenly as it had started, the commercial was over. I thought about the wooden keychain cross still hidden in my bag. I felt Emma tugging on my leg and looked down at her smiling up at me, the now disconnected phone dangling from her tiny hand.

Suddenly, Jeff's voice broke through the silence as he strode through the door. "Hey, hey, hey!" he announced. "I'm home!" Emma beamed and ran to reach him. "Daaadddeeee!" He reached down and scooped her up.

"How was everyone's day?" he asked.

With the words from the song giving me the courage I needed, I walked over to my teacher bag, pulled out the small

Chapter Ten: Gifts

piece of tissue, and unwrapped the wooden cross keychain. I extended my hand so that Jeff and Emma could see it.

"I think I want to go to church," I said, looking up at him.

He looked from the keychain to me for just a moment, and then a smile spread across his face. "Geez, I was only a few minutes late, what happened while I was gone!?" he laughed.

Chapter Eleven

Church

After Emma went to bed that night, Jeff and I sat down on the couch in our living room for a long-overdue talk. Over the next few hours, I told him everything. I told him about the hallway prayer, the Bible verses on Sharon's and Rob's desks, the secret gifts, "Shout to the Lord," and how I had bowed my head to pray in front of my students. His eyes grew wider with each new detail. When I finished telling my story, Jeff looked at me sadly.

"Why didn't you tell me?" I could've helped you, we could have gotten through it together."

I looked down at my hands, hoping he'd understand what I was about to say. "I didn't want you to think I was weak," I started. "And to be honest, I didn't want to say any of it out loud because that would make everything real, and I'm still not sure what I'm going to do with all of this. But I have to find out."

He paused thoughtfully, "You know, I don't think I've ever had a hallway moment like you had."

"I want you to have one! Emma, too." I said hopefully. "I want that for our family."

Chapter Eleven: Church

"Hmmmm, well, what do you want to do with all of this?" he asked.

"I want to go to church," I said, smiling resolutely.

"What kind of church?"

"Sharon and a lot of the teachers go to Riverside Church. It's in an elementary school."

He paused for a long moment. "Cara, what are you going to tell your parents?"

I paused too, feeling a weight settle on my chest. "I don't know, but everything in my heart is pushing me forward. I can't walk away from this. I'm hoping going to church will give me answers."

He looked at me with admiration, "Ok, then it's decided. We're going to church!" He wrapped me in a bear hug, and I felt the weight lift.

Suddenly, he pulled away and looked me seriously in the eyes, startling me. "I have one more important question."

"What?" I asked nervously.

"Do I have to get dressed up for this church?" I punched him lightly on the arm as he grinned back at me.

The next morning, I talked to Sharon about her church and about the song, "Shout to the Lord."

"I LOOOOOVVVE that song!" she said enthusiastically. "We sing it during worship!"

"Do you think Jeff, Emma, and I could come on Sunday?" I asked.

"Cara Shine!" She clapped her hands together. "Uh, yesssssss!" she exclaimed. "Of course! You're going to know so many people from school. Emma can go to the nursery if you want. I'll introduce you to our Pastor, Brian Clark, too!"

I wasn't sure I was ready for all that, especially putting Emma in a nursery with strangers. It was going to take all my courage to just walk through the doors. But I nodded my head as she confirmed that Jeff did not need to get dressed up.

I tossed and turned on Saturday night, but Sunday morning was full of sunlight. I stood inside my closet and stared at the clothes in my closet trying to decide what to wear. If this were my hometown synagogue, I would know what to expect. Everyone would be dressed respectfully, the service would flow from the beginning call to worship of the *Barchu*, to the voice of the Cantor leading us in melodic song, and then the Rabbi leading us in the *Shema*. But I had no idea what a church service in an elementary school gymnasium would look like, or if the feeling I desperately wanted to share with Jeff and Emma would even be present, but I hoped so.

I settled on dress pants and a button-down shirt, dressier than I probably needed, but if I really was about to meet Jesus, I didn't want to be underdressed. I put Emma in a baby blue pair of leggings, a matching jumper, and patent leather shoes. Jeff was very happy to be in his comfortable khakis. Emma was thrilled to be going anywhere with us that included being outside since we'd been trapped inside for almost three weeks now, so she was smiling and kicking her feet against her car seat as she juggled a small ball along to a song by The Wiggles, "Hot Potato, Hot Potato."

As we pulled out of the driveway, Jeff had to stop to let Sheku pass behind us as she headed out for the day, too. Since the kids weren't allowed to play outside anymore, our afternoon front yard chats had stopped. I missed her sage advice.

Although I had gone to college with other Muslims, Sheku was the first Muslim that I thought to ask about her faith. We would sit in her sunroom, watching Emma play, drinking coffee, and talking about both our faiths openly, both of us trying to get to the heart of it all. I decided she would be my

Chapter Eleven: Church

first phone call after church.

Riverside Church was only ten minutes away, and Jeff glanced over at me at a stoplight to smile, giving me the courage I needed to breathe slowly and repeat my prayers. "Fear not. Do not be afraid," and "Be still and know that I am God." I let the familiar and comforting words of the *Shema* speak to me as well. I longed for the two parts of my oddly shaped spiritual puzzle to somehow magically fit together.

We arrived early, which was good because within minutes, the parking lot was full. One by one, I watched as people got out of their cars and walked up the sidewalk. Some were walking quickly, ushering their families inside as fast as possible, others walked slowly and intently, and some walked in zigzag lines, but everyone continued walking towards the church.

Jeff sensed my apprehension and offered me his hand. "You ready?" he asked.

"Yes." But the truth was, both my mind and my heart were racing. We got Emma out of her car seat and began walking towards the front door. But after a few steps, my resolve began to fade. *You don't belong here. Everyone is going to know you don't belong here. You should get back in the car.*

And then I saw a sign, just outside the front doors. It was a foldable sandwich board sign with the words *Welcome, Everyone* in bold teal letters. The faces of my bullies flashed through my mind, but I focused on the words on the sign instead. *Welcome, EVERYONE.* That included me.

As promised, Sharon was waiting in the foyer along with her husband Mike and their two girls, Elaine and Alyssa. As the girls made a fuss over Emma, Mike and Jeff fell into an easy conversation about the football game that was on later that day. Sharon pulled me aside for, "Just a quick minute." We stepped off to a quiet corner, and she handed me a beautiful, but heavy gift bag.

"What's this?" I asked.

"Just open it," she said giddily.

The white tissue paper crinkled in my hands as I moved each piece aside to reveal a deep maroon colored Bible. In gold letters across the spine, it read, *NIV Study Bible.*

"Well," she smiled deeply. "You keep peeking at my desk calendar anyway, so I thought maybe you'd like to read the whole thing for yourself!" Her eyes twinkled. The Bible caught me off guard, which registered on my face, chasing Sharon's smile away. "Oh gosh," she stammered. "I hope that wasn't too forward of me."

I felt awful for my reaction, but I knew why. I was waging a fierce war in my head, trying to reconcile my two worlds.

I reached out and gave Sharon a hug. "No, Sharon. I love it, really. It's perfect," I said, hoping she'd forgive me.

"Ok," she said, a tentative smile returning to her face. "Well, there's still one more thing left in the bag for you." I reached back into the bag and carefully removed the rest of the paper to reveal a blue CD case that read, "WOW Worship, Today's 30 Most Powerful Worship Songs."

"Shout to the Lord is track number seven," she winked, as a genuine look of joy spread across my face. She turned to both our families, who were growing restless. "Come on, we'd better head in before all the seats are gone!"

Before I could thank her, she grabbed me by the hand and led us into the school gymnasium, where hundreds of plastic chairs were already filled with people. A large make-shift stage and huge, drop-down screen were stationed at the front of the room. And in the middle of the stage was a rock band complete with a guitarist, a bassist, and a drummer. This was, in my opinion, a far cry from the holiness of the *Bema* at my synagogue that housed the Torah. *I've made a huge mistake,* I thought, and looked quickly to the exit, trying to decide how

Chapter Eleven: Church

I could get all three of us out of there before it was too late.

But that's when I saw Lauren, one of my favorite students from years ago, up on the stage and part of the band. I hadn't seen her in years, and sweet memories of our time together in the classroom brought back lovely memories. I suddenly remembered Lauren talking about church activities on Monday mornings as the students discussed their weekends. Her family must have been attending Riverside for a long time. I decided to stay, just to see Lauren.

Sharon led us to the row she had saved for us and, true to her word, I saw several familiar teacher faces immediately. We settled into the seats, and Jeff and I made eye contact. I could see he was unsure about all this as well, but we were in too deep to leave now.

Suddenly, a man took the stage and walked up to the microphone. I assumed he was part of the band since he was dressed in comfy khakis too, but he was, to my surprise, the Pastor.

"Hi everyone! Welcome to Riverside Church. If it's your first time here, we're so glad you're here. Will you stand and join us in worship on this beautiful Sunday morning?"

The lights were dimmed, the band started playing, and the entire gymnasium stood up. The screen lit up with words to a song. I wanted to run for the door, or hide, or just crawl under my seat. Was this a rock concert or a church? Until I saw the title of the song flash up on the screen in bold black words. "Shine, Jesus, Shine." I squinted to make sure I was seeing it correctly; I was. Jeff, Sharon, and I locked eyes in disbelief as the band and my sweet student, Lauren, tore down my walls with my very own last name.

Lauren's voice was pure and beautiful. I looked down at Emma, who was taking all of this in and watching all the other children in the row with wide eyes, too. Some people were clapping to the music, others swaying, and everyone was singing, jubilantly! I was certain they didn't all know each other, but they were still completely surrendered and united as they sang to Jesus. It reminded me of the *WOW CD* commercial I had seen. An intense spirit pressed into my heart, causing the hairs on my arms to stand up.

The *warmth* returned. I reached for both Jeff and Emma's hands, willing it to spread into their hearts too.

As the song came to an end, Pastor Brian took the stage. I followed everyone's lead and sat back down. I felt dizzy and overwhelmed. I wondered what Jeff was thinking. Pastor Brian broke the tension of the moment with a joke about his favorite football team, the Philadelphia Eagles, and I could feel Jeff relax. Pastor Brian spoke with the casualness of a next-door neighbor, making it easy to lean into his words.

"I know, today, many of you are living in fear for different reasons. Maybe you're facing a medical fear, or an economic fear, or a fear about your children's safety. But I think it's safe to say that we all experience fear at some point in our lives. And with hundreds of law enforcement agents working around the clock to capture a sniper, and our children unable to play outside safely, it would be easy for us to lose hope. Raise your hand if you're feeling a little fearful these days."

Every hand in the room shot up, including mine. Pastor Brian smiled and nodded as he responded to our collective need with compassion. "Me too. But the good news of Christ is that we don't have to live in fear. Our living hope gives us the courage to face challenging times, and this community provides us with opportunities to connect, empower, and impact each other with Christ's love." I turned to Jeff to see what he thought of all this, but our eyes didn't meet; he was laser-focused on Pastor Brian. I reached for his hand instead.

Pastor Brian continued, "I'm going to call my eldest son, Daniel, up here with me." A blonde, teenage boy with an infectious smile stood up and made his way to the stage to stand next to Pastor Brian. "Many of you know Daniel already, and I think many of you like him," the crowd murmured kindly and nodded.

He continued, "Well, that's something we can agree on. We all love Dan." Dan grinned at both the congregation and his father. Pastor Brian paused. "But do you love him enough to die for him?" A hush settled over the gymnasium. Pastor Brian smiled. "I would never ask you to, so you can relax."

The tension lifted from the room. Brian continued. "I would, though. With no second thought. I would take the bullet intended for Dan—he's my son. But I have to be honest, if that bullet was intended for one of you, and I had a choice, to save you, I'm not sure the decision would be that easy. As your Pastor, I hope I'd do the right thing and choose to save you, but the truth is, I'm a human and prone to self-preservation, so I'd give it a 50/50 chance." We all shifted uncomfortably in our seats.

"As much as I love each of you, I am still just a human. Saving someone in my family, you bet. Saving someone outside of my family, hmmmm." Jeff and I looked at each other. What kind of Pastor was this?

Brian spoke again, "But here's the good news, Jesus would take the bullet for you. In fact, he has already made that sacrifice. When he died a sinner's death as an innocent man, he did that for you because he considers you his family." Emma crawled up on my lap to snuggle, and I squeezed her tightly to my chest. You could hear a pin drop throughout the gymnasium.

"It would be easy to say that Jesus didn't give it a second thought, but the tears he cried in the Garden of Gethsemane show that he suffered greatly. And he knew his sacrifice was going to be horrible. Horrific, and he did it anyway. For you."

Pastor Brian paused for a moment. I thought maybe he'd forgotten what he was going to say, until I realized he was fighting back emotions. "That's how Jesus feels about you. And the evidence of that love hangs on the cross."

The weight of these words hit me like an anvil. I imagined the nails being driven into Jesus' hands and feet as his mother watched helplessly. *THIS*, I thought, *THIS is the real Jesus.*

"Friends, these past three weeks, living in our area has been hard. But I'm here to tell you that God has left a spirit of hope within you, not fear. Jesus didn't die so that you would live a life of anxiety. He died so that you could live. Really live! His greatest desire is for you to walk with him so that everyone who meets you feels his grace."

"That doesn't mean there won't be hard times or seasons of suffering, it just means we don't have to go it alone, and we have scripture to lean on for strength. And we also have each other to care for one another, and most importantly, to pray for each other. Let's look at what the Bible tells us about fear."

The entire congregation reached for their Bibles. But before I had a chance to reach for my new Bible, the words of the verses flashed across the screen for everyone to see. A small gasp escaped my lips.

"Fear not, for I am with you; Be not dismayed, for I am your God. I will strengthen you, Yes, I will help you, I will uphold you with My righteous right hand." (Isaiah 41:10 NKJV)

I couldn't believe it—it was my verse! It felt like a series of mini miracles, and the beginning of a new story written just for me, by God.

But as we sat in church, the FBI broke a story of their own. An anonymous caller claiming to be the sniper called the tip hotline to "brag" about a murder he had committed in Montgomery, Alabama, a month earlier. A quick-thinking agent decided to pursue the lead and unearthed a vital piece of evidence. But not before 37-year-old Jeffrey Hopper was shot and wounded after leaving a Ponderosa steakhouse in Ashland, Virginia, and a few days later, on October 22, 35-year-old Conrad Johnson was fatally shot while standing on the top step of the commuter bus he was driving.

Chapter Twelve

Matthew

I called Sheku as soon as we got home from church and told her I had something important to share with her. She invited me to come over as soon as I could; she'd get the coffee going. Jeff took Emma to the basement to run off some extra energy before her nap.

Jeff and I hadn't had much time to download everything that happened at church, but he'd told me everything I needed to know with one simple sentence as we exited the elementary school. "I'd go back there again," he'd said, grabbing both our hands to cross the parking lot. "Even though there was a lot of singing," he'd grinned.

But I had loved the singing. In fact, I loved everything about church. It would have been easy to dismiss Lauren singing, "Shine, Jesus, Shine" and then the "Fear not," verse as a coincidence, but I couldn't.

I changed into my fuzzy sweatpants and walked next door to Sheku's house, admiring the bright yellow mums and huge pumpkins that decorated her front stoop. Everything about her home said, "Welcome, Everyone," too. As I stood on her doorstep, waiting for her to answer the doorbell, I realized I wasn't panicked about being exposed and out in the open. My zig-zagging had disappeared.

Sheku opened the door and embraced me with a smile and a hug. Her home was full of trinkets, memories, and the most delicious smells imaginable. True to her word, she'd brewed a delicious pot of coffee, complete with steamed milk and a dusting of cinnamon sprinkled over the top. I cradled my mug as we walked to our favorite spot, her sunroom. It was an oasis of dark colored rugs, comfy couches filled with pillows, and even a rope swing. We tucked our legs underneath us, crisscross, and settled in.

"Soooo," she began. "What's new?" Out of all my friends, I knew only Sheku could understand the weight of what I was about to say.

When the planes hit the Twin Towers on 9/11, she mourned the senseless loss of so many lives. But Sheku also had to mourn for the future of her family. As Muslim Americans, they had been lumped into an overgeneralized, hateful version of their faith with a new name: Terrorists. There were constant sideways glances from strangers, triple security checks when they flew, and hurtful words, reminiscent of my school bus memories. Jeff took Sheku flowers after 9/11 as a reminder that we loved her, but it didn't change the truth of her new reality.

I took a deep breath and looked her in the eyes. "We went to church today." Her eyes grew as wide as the mug she was holding.

"You went to church?" she repeated, to make sure she'd heard me correctly.

"Yes," I said calmly. She put her coffee mug down on the table and shifted her legs so she could face me better.

"Why?" she asked incredulously.

I paused for a moment, unsure of how to answer her question. There was no sane answer. I couldn't answer her "why" question. But I could explain how.

As I began describing the Bible verses, the hallway prayer, the gifts, and the songs at church, she leaned in closer to absorb it all. And then I reached into my purse to show her the wooden cross that now hung from my keyring.

"It was the most beautiful feeling I've ever felt, Sheku," I described. "A whole room filled with hope and joy, and God was at the center of it all." Her face softened as I described the rest of the service, including Communion.

"The Pastor said EVERYONE was welcome to receive Communion."

"Did you go up?" she asked tentatively.

"No," I said, "We stayed in our seats. But hundreds of others did." I thought I noticed a shift behind her eyes.

"Have you told your parents?" A deep furrow developed between her eyes.

I paused, "No, not yet. I don't know how."

She settled back onto the pillows of the couch. "Oh, Cara, this is hard. You and I both come from a people that are immovable on certain things, don't we? What you're asking might be too much for a lot of your family and friends." My heart sank.

"But that shouldn't keep you from this journey. If you feel God is pursuing you through Jesus, I think your only choice is to find out everything you can about Him. Then you can decide for yourself what comes next. If you stop exploring now, you'll always wonder." I thought about my new Bible sitting at home on the kitchen island.

"Just make sure you are 100% certain before you tell them." She paused, seeming to start and then stop what she was about to say.

Chapter Twelve: Matthew

"What?" I asked, sensing a shift in her mood.

Another pause. "No, I just think you're incredibly brave. I don't think I could ever do what you're doing." *Brave*. It was a word I'd never used to describe myself before.

We hugged, I promised to keep her in the loop, and I headed back home expecting Emma to be awake from her nap.

But she wasn't, and Jeff had fallen asleep in his comfy khakis on the living room couch. I reached for the gift bag on the island, making sure the tissue paper didn't shift noisily, and carried it upstairs to the bedroom. The sun was peeking through the side window, illuminating a corner of the room. I reached into the bag, pulled out the Bible, and sat on the floor facing the sun.

The Bible smelled of fresh leather, and the binding cracked a bit as I opened it. My fingers had to adjust to the thinness of each page, delicate and fragile, just like the tissue paper. The table of contents revealed the five books of the Torah that I knew: Genesis, Exodus, Leviticus, Numbers, and Deuteronomy, along with the other books of the Old Testament that I had never taken the time to read for myself. I vowed to go back and read them all. I turned the page to reveal what I had come for: The New Testament.

The Book of Matthew began on page 1463. As I read the study notes before the chapter, my heart soared when I realized that the author, Matthew, was a Jew, just like me, with everything to lose and nothing to gain if he followed Jesus. He was a tax collector, who must have been hated by his own people for working with the Roman government, and was no role model. And yet, Jesus chose him. A sinner, just like me, just like the kids on the bus, just like everyone.

I read as Matthew described Jesus' genealogy, tracing Him as a direct descendant from the House of David, and then flipped back to the Book of Jeremiah to read the Messianic prophecy.

"The days are coming," declares the Lord, "when I will raise up for David a righteous Branch, a King who will reign wisely and do what is just and right in the land." (Jeremiah 23:5 NIV) I read about the virgin birth and followed the study notes to Isaiah 7:14, "Therefore the Lord himself will give you a sign: The virgin will conceive and will give birth to a son, and will call him Immanuel." (Isaiah 7:14 NIV), and how Jesus was born in Bethlehem. "But you, Bethlehem, Ephrathah, though you are small among the clans of Judah, out of you will come for me one who will be ruler over Israel, whose origins are from of old, from ancient times." (Micah 5:2 NIV) And in the same corner of the bedroom where I'd spiraled with anxiety, now I sat reading the words of Jesus.

"One of them, an expert in the law, tested him with this question: "Teacher, which is the greatest commandment in the Law?" Jesus replied: "Love the Lord your God with all your heart and with all your soul and with all your mind. This is the first and greatest commandment. And the second is like it: 'Love your neighbor as yourself.' All the Law and Prophets hang on these two commandments." (Matthew 22:35-40 NIV)

My heart skipped a beat; this was the *Shema*! The prayer of my people! Jesus loved the *Shema*, too? Jesus must have stood in his synagogue, shoulder to shoulder with other Jews, reciting this sacred prayer just like me. I looked up to the sunlight; tears running openly down my face, and spoke the name I'd been running from for years outloud. *JESUS.*

Chapter Thirteen

Caught

As I sat on the floor in the little corner of my bedroom, letting the words of Jesus capture my heart, FBI agents broke the Beltway Sniper case wide open. The hot-line tip yielded a match. Fingerprints and ballistic evidence from a gun magazine dropped at one of the shootings matched prints that were already on file in the Alabama case. The match was for sixteen-year-old Lee Boyd Malvo, who already had a criminal record. The same arrest record also provided another name: 41-year-old John Allen Muhammad, an ex-Army sergeant who had a Bushmaster .223 rifle registered in his name, which was a federal violation of a restraining order filed by his ex-wife. John Muhammad also had a blue Chevy Caprice with New Jersey plates. There were, in fact, two snipers, not one. On October 22, the FBI released the details of the two men and their car, asking the public to be on the lookout.

The morning of October 24 began in the same way it had for me for weeks, with my radio alarm clock. But this time, before my radio could hand me a song for the day, another song was already playing in my head, "Shout to the Lord." The lyrics carried me through my morning routine, getting Emma dressed, and all the way downstairs to make her breakfast. And that's what was playing in my head when Jeff called down to us, from upstairs.

"They caught them!"

"What?" I yelled back, closing the refrigerator door and leaning closer to the staircase so I could hear him better.

Jeff hurried down the stairs still in his pajamas, "Turn on the TV! They caught the snipers!"

We both rushed to the television and turned on the local news. It was on every station, John Allen Muhammad and Lee Boyd Malvo had been caught at 3:30 A.M. that morning as they slept inside their blue Chevy Caprice. They had been parked at a rest stop off I-70 in Maryland when quick-thinking civilians spotted the car and called the police.

Shocking pictures from inside the car flashed across the screen. The snipers had turned their car into a mobile sniper's nest by removing parts of the back seat and trunk and drilling an opening just wide enough for a rifle near the back license plate. Police also found a .223 Bush Master rifle, a tripod, walkie-talkies, a laptop stolen from one of the victims, maps of the shooting sites and getaway routes, and more.

We stood in the living room, hanging on every detail while Emma sat happily at the kitchen table, eating her waffles as if nothing had changed. But it had. Everything had changed. The relief I felt was palpable. Jeff gave me a big hug and whispered, "I hope you can relax now. Want to go for a long walk outside after dinner tonight?"

"Absolutely!" I smiled back. But in the back of my head, I knew I couldn't relax until I did one more thing. I still needed to tell my parents about Jesus.

Chapter Fourteen

Tom

But months went by, and I simply couldn't find the courage. I was distracted by the return of recess, evening walks, and the freedom to live again. Each sunrise was sweeter, each sunset more beautiful, and I promised myself I would never take "outside" for granted again. Both Muhammed and Malvo were found guilty on multiple counts of murder. Malvo received multiple life sentences without the possibility of parole. Muhammed received the death penalty.

The fall leaves turned into winter snow that blanketed the nation's Capital and seemed to heal the invisible wounds left behind from snipers' bullets. Everything felt different, and I looked at the world with a new set of eyes. Each morning, I woke not with a sense of dread, but with one of hope. And every Sunday, the three of us went to church.

Pastor Brian had spoken about this feeling in church one Sunday, calling it, "The peace that surpasses all understanding," just like Sharon had said in that hallway prayer. Now it all made sense. I nodded my head in agreement with the congregation as I marveled at the irony of what had brought me to church in the first place.

Each Sunday, I sat in my chair with Emma either on my

lap or playing at my feet, feeling like a sponge. Everything was new to me: the flow of the service, the time of greeting, the entire New Testament, and especially Communion. I still hadn't been able to walk forward when Pastor Brian invited the congregation up, even though he made it abundantly clear that "This table is for everyone. A small voice in my head added, "not yet," each week. Always taking my lead, Jeff waited too, not wanting to leave me seated in the row alone.

We started attending Riverside's "new member" class to learn more about the church and to talk with Pastor Brian one-on-one. I was struck by his humility, his intelligence, and his love for Jesus. Each week, he'd listen thoughtfully as I posed question after question about the New Testament. *How did the Trinity work? How could Jesus be both man and God at the same time? Why did God allow bad things to happen to good people?* He always made time for my calls and prayed with Jeff and me often.

As Christmas approached, I grew increasingly excited. I couldn't wait to celebrate the birth of Jesus for the very first time, so I announced to Jeff one Saturday morning, "I want a Christmas tree!" In true Jeff fashion, he jumped right on board, dropped what he was doing, and headed to Home Depot to pick out our first Christmas tree while Emma and I went to shop for decorations.

But as I stood in the middle of the Christmas aisle at Target, I realized I had no idea what to buy, beginning with Christmas tree lights. There seemed to be thousands of choices. Should I get tiny, twinkly lights or large, multi-colored ones? Did I need a string of 500 bulbs or 100? How was I supposed to know? Hanukkah Menorahs were much easier to navigate. Emma ran up and down the aisles, delighted by everything as she picked up ornament after ornament.

"Mommy! Mommy, woooookk, it's Hunter," Ms. Susan's golden labrador. I lifted her up so she could place her very first ornament into our shopping cart.

Chapter Fourteen: Tom

Confused and overwhelmed, I grabbed one box of tiny lights and decided to give up. We were headed to the check-out line when something in the Christmas clearance section caught my eye: a green ceramic cross hanging from a red ribbon. I picked it up gingerly.

Emma clapped her hands and exclaimed, "Ohhhh, Mommy, that's Jesus," as she extended a tiny finger to trace the etchings of the delicate ornament. My heart soared. I placed the cross lovingly into the cart. I guess I wasn't the only one who had been absorbing grace on Sunday mornings.

Over the next month, I navigated buying lots of other Christmas decorations for the house and made a lot of rookie Christian mistakes. I must have made a hundred trips back and forth to Target. I bought a beautiful Christmas wreath with a huge maroon bow for our front door before realizing I also needed a hook to hang it on. I bought fake green garland for our hallway banisters that were too short, then exchanged them for ones that were too long. I eventually just hand-tied them in a knot and gave up. Martha Stewart would have been horrified, but I was proud of myself.

I also asked a lot of questions about Santa Claus. It seemed unfair that Jeff and I would be the ones to put in all the work, and then the guy in a white beard and red suit would get all the credit. And what about the Christmas cookie and milk thing? Wasn't that just doubling down on a lie I already felt bad about? When I posed this question in the teacher's lounge to several other friends, they said, "You're not lying, you're just pretending for her benefit!"

And in the end, they were right. It was all worth it. The look on Emma's face when she came downstairs on Christmas morning was pure magic. We took a picture in front of the Christmas tree with the green ceramic cross hanging proudly from the branches.

My parents had plans to visit us in January, so as soon

as Christmas was over, I packed everything away before their visit. My mom arrived with a box of assorted games and arts and crafts projects to entertain Emma for hours, and my dad brought his toolbox to help Jeff fix whatever needed to be repaired around the house. It was a lovely visit, except for the big thing I was hiding in my heart. I wanted to tell them about my newfound joy, and about grace, and about Jesus. But instead, I kept it all to myself, still unable to find the right words.

"Cara, you can't keep this up forever," Jeff said as my parents backed out of the driveway for the eight-hour drive back to Ohio. I knew he was right; something had to give soon. Pastor Brian encouraged me to pray for strength and courage. I prayed every night that God would present an opportunity for a conversation that would build bridges, not walls, between us.

The winter snow slowly melted into spring days, and we exchanged our heavy sweaters for light jackets. Emma played outside with the rest of the neighborhood kids after school, and every chance I got, I sat in the corner of my bedroom, consuming the New Testament like it was the air I breathed.

After finishing the Book of Matthew, I moved on to the other gospels, reading Mark, then Luke, and finally the Book of John. I was struck by how each gospel told the same story, even though they'd been written separately and without the benefit of email or telephone to cross-reference each account.

And within the first few verses of the Book of John, the two things I loved the most, my Jewish identity and Jesus, finally found a home big enough for both to live. "In the beginning was the Word, and the Word was with God, and the Word was God. He was with God in the beginning. Through him all things were made; without him nothing was made that has been made. In him was life, and that life was the light of all mankind. The light shines in the darkness, and the darkness has not overcome it." (John 1:1-5 NIV)

Chapter Fourteen: Tom

There it was. Jesus was both WITH God and IN God. From our first breath to our last, Jesus and God were the same. When I stood with my Jewish friends at a sleep-away camp, when Jeff stepped on the glass at our wedding, when Emma was born, God and Jesus had been there, together. There was no need to keep God and Jesus separate in my heart; I could love them both. And so, I decided, I wanted to celebrate the new life Jesus had given me. I wanted to be baptized, and I wanted that for Emma, too.

Jeff and I met with Brian, and we picked a date: Sunday, April 27, 2003. I asked Sharon if she would stand next to me. She hugged me and exclaimed, "Oh, honey! Nothing would make me happier!" Word spread quickly, and many of my friends said they wanted to be there as well.

I invited Sheku, too. She was family to me, and I sat in her sunroom for hours that winter, sharing what I was reading in the Bible as she listened intently, questioning and processing with me. I hoped she would come, but understood that attending a Christian baptism might be too hard.

The week before our baptism, I took Emma to the mall and bought her a simple white dress. She looked so sweet, even though she announced that it was "scwatchy." I tried to remain focused at work, but I couldn't stop thinking about Sunday. I vacillated between joy and guilt; I wished my parents could be there, too.

When I picked Emma up from Susan's house that Friday, I continued the conversation I had been having with her all week, so she'd be ready in two days' time.

"Em, do you remember what we're doing this Sunday at church?" I asked, looking back at her in the rearview mirror. I was amazed at how tall she'd grown since October. There was no way I would be able to play Kangaroo with her anymore. I thanked God that I no longer needed to. He was in control.

"Yes, Mommy! Baptazeee Day. For Jesus!" she smiled, but then quickly scowled. "I don't want to wear the dress." Her little eyebrows got tight as she tried to look angry, but it only made me laugh.

"I know, but it's a special day, and I'll be wearing a dress, too. We can go out for lunch afterwards, and you can get butter noodles and French fries. Her face brightened again.

As we pulled into the house, I was already thinking of the long list of things I wanted to accomplish that evening: start a load of laundry, iron Emma's dress, and figure out what to make for dinner. I considered chicken parmesan. I was surprised to see that Jeff had beaten us home from work. He greeted us at the door, sweeping Emma up into a bear hug and carrying her inside as they made plans to head outside right after dinner to play ball. I dropped my teacher bag down, just as the phone rang. Jeff adjusted Emma in his arms and picked it up.

"Hello? Oh, hey, Sam! What's up?" I moved to the refrigerator to double-check that I had all the ingredients I needed for dinner, but a sudden long silence caught my attention. Jeff had stopped talking. I looked from behind the refrigerator door to find him.

Jeff had stopped smiling.

I froze, leaving the refrigerator door half-opened. Jeff wasn't moving; he was just listening intently to Sam.

Emma sensed the shift in her Daddy, too, and stopped squirming in his arms. She reached out and tenderly touched his face with her hands, searching for his smile. She looked back at me, confused.

"When?" he asked Sam, as he moved to put Emma down gently, and then turned and walked down the hallway, head down.

Chapter Fourteen: Tom

Emma walked over and took my hand, scanning my face, too. I could feel my heart beating faster. I reached down and picked her up, hugging her, but saying nothing. I shut the refrigerator door and followed Jeff into the office.

He was sitting down at the desk, both hands on his knees. I held my breath and waited.

He looked up at me.

"Cara, Tom's dead."

Chapter Fifteen

Red Light

I didn't move. I couldn't. I wanted to erase the sentence Jeff had just spoken. "Tom's dead." If I could just rewind to the minute before the phone rang, we could live in that version of reality, a reality where Tom was still alive.

"No," I said, hoping my words would make it true.

"He's gone, Cara. He died this morning; he had a diabetic seizure in his sleep."

"No," I repeated.

Jeff moved closer to me, but I moved away. Emma moved towards us both.

She lifted her arms up. "Daddy, up?" she asked sweetly. Jeff leaned over and raised her into his arms. She melted into the crook of his neck, trying to console him, sensing his hurt. It was too much for me.

"I have to go," I said, as I turned around abruptly. I didn't want Emma to see me fall apart again. I walked back to the kitchen, grabbed my keys, and ran to my car, blind to everything I was leaving behind. I slammed the car door, threw it in reverse, and sped out of the driveway. I wanted to get as far away from Jeff's words as I could. I hit the gas.

Chapter Fifteen: Red Light

As I approached the intersection leading out of the neighborhood, the red light changed to green. *Good,* I thought, *I just want to drive and drive and drive.* The same thing happened at the next intersection, another green light. A series of green lights, one after another, allowed me to get further away from what Jeff had said, "Tom's dead."

I logged more miles. Why would Jesus allow this? I thought He loved us like His own. Weren't all His plans supposed to work for our good? I couldn't stop thinking about Tom's parents.

I thought about how I'd forgotten to call Tom back twice. Why had I been so selfishly wrapped up in my own world?

I hit every green light, one after another, after another. The irony of a string of green lights as I cried uncontrollably only made me angrier with Jesus. If this was how Jesus rewarded His people, two days before our Baptism, maybe I'd been wrong about it all, maybe I'd been wrong about Him. What kind of love would steal Tom away from us, from his friends and his family at the age of 32?

I couldn't hold it in anymore, I screamed out loud, "Why? Why would you do this?"

The silence in the car made me feel so alone. I wanted Jesus' attention, so I threw down the only gauntlet I had. "If you really love us all so much, then show me a sign, or I'm walking away!"

As soon as the challenge left my lips, I regretted it immediately. It was blasphemous. Who was I to demand anything of Jesus?

I needed to stop thinking; if I could just stop thinking, I could pull myself together. I needed a distraction, as Sheku suggested. Music would help.

I remembered the *WOW Worship* CD that Sharon had given me months ago on my first day at church. I had put it in the glove box and forgotten all about it. The light at the next intersection turned red, giving me enough time to open the glove box, tear off the cellophane wrapper, and push the CD into the player. I could hear the CD player queuing up the next random selection. But before the music played, the light turned green, and I looked up at the car in front of me for the first time.

I gasped out loud and gripped the steering wheel as I leaned in closer to make sure I wasn't seeing things. I wasn't. The license plate of the car that had been sitting right in front of me as I screamed at Jesus for a sign read, "WVU-TM." West Virginia University, Tom.

I blinked again, trying to be sure of what I was seeing. I heard one honk, and then another. The cars behind me grew impatient, but I couldn't move. I didn't want to move. I looked around to find someone who could be a witness to what I was seeing. But there was no one.

But Jesus is here, a small voice in my head echoed. *Jesus has always been here.*

I was never more certain of the presence of Jesus than in that moment. I had asked, and Jesus had answered.

And as I slowly took my foot off the brake and finally moved my car forward, the *WOW* CD clicked and settled on its randomized selection. I heard the first few notes of the song that had started it all, as "Shout to the Lord," played throughout my car and Jesus rushed into my heart.

God hadn't given me just one sign—He had given me two.

Chapter Sixteen

Green Light

At the next possible intersection, I turned the car around and headed straight home. I pulled back into the driveway, jumped out of the car, and ran inside the house calling for Jeff. He was downstairs in the basement playing with Emma, but his smile was still gone. A wave of guilt washed over me as I realized that I shouldn't have left him alone.

But as I told him about what had happened at the red light, all of that disappeared. I recounted the story two more times to make sure I didn't leave anything out. It was almost unbelievable, but it had happened. God had provided. As we hugged each other tightly, Emma stopped chasing her ball and joined us, wrapping her arms around both of our legs. My heart broke knowing she'd grow up without Tom, but I knew when she was old enough to understand, I would keep his memory alive by telling her the story of how, at a red light, Jesus had given me a miracle.

It seemed like the wrong time to celebrate anything, especially a baptism. I wasn't sure I could go through with it just two days after losing Tom. We called Pastor Brian for help, and without giving it a second thought, he offered to come over to pray with us.

The basement was too dark, so we decided to go outside to wait for him. Emma carried the mini soccer ball that Tom had given her up the stairs. She was delighted to see Sheku weeding the garden in her front yard when we stepped outside.

"Sheeeeekuuuuu!" she yelled. "Come play!" But as soon as Sheku saw us, she sensed our sadness.

"Cara, what's going on?" she asked softly. She drew her head close to mine as I shared our pain.

And just as I finished telling her everything, Pastor Brian pulled into the driveway. But rather than leave, Sheku stayed with us and listened quietly as Brian talked with us about grief, the promise of eternal life with Jesus, and the beauty of baptism.

Brian offered, "I know your hearts are heavy, but if you're thinking of ways to honor Tom, linking your new life in Christ to Tom's new life in heaven seems like a wonderful thing. It won't bring him back, but it will bind your memories together forever. Let's pray for Tom now." He reached out his hands for us to join in a circle.

Without thinking, I grabbed Sheku's hand too, and together we prayed for Tom in our front yard as cars and neighbors passed by. But as we opened our eyes, I could see that Sheku seemed unsettled; our prayer circle had made her uncomfortable. She gave me a quick hug, excused herself, and headed back home. I felt horrible—the last thing I wanted was to make her feel uncomfortable, especially after all she'd done for me. I offered up a small prayer. *God, move in Sheku's heart, too. Protect her, please.* I watched as she headed inside her house.

Brian turned to leave, too, but stopped short before getting in his car. "Cara, since you're moving forward with the baptism on Sunday, if you haven't already come clean to your parents yet, maybe this is your sign." I knew he was right — life was too short and too precious.

So, on Saturday morning, the day before our baptism, I decided it was time to call them. I sat in the corner of my bedroom, now my favorite place to talk to God, and asked for courage. I prayed for the right words and asked Jesus to fill the conversation with the Holy Spirit. His answer to my prayer was clear: "Fear not, do not be afraid."

But my heart still raced as I picked up the phone and dialed their number. My mom answered first.

"Hi Mom, can you get Dad on the phone? I need to tell you something," I could hear her pause and then call out to my father. There was some muffled conversation on their end that I couldn't make out. And then, to my surprise, they spoke first.

"Cara, we already know what you're about to tell us. Emma told us a few months ago. Say what you need to say. We love you."

I was stunned into silence. Apparently, on several occasions, when I'd handed the phone over to Emma so she could talk with them *pwivatly,* she'd told them that we'd been going to church. They'd made a point of calling on Sundays for several weeks, just to be sure. My sweet girl had unknowingly given each of us time to process everything on our own. Without me knowing, God had been working behind the scenes the whole time; I only needed to "Be still."

"Dad, Mom, I can't explain it. But I've never felt happier. I guess the word I really mean is joyful. And I feel complete."

There was a long silence on the other end of the phone. Then my dad spoke, "We want you to be happy. We love you. But we just don't understand. Why do you want to follow them, after everything they've done to us?"

The confusion and sadness in their voices broke my heart. And just like when Sheku had asked me the same question in her sunroom, I knew I needed to share the Jesus I'd met in the hallway with them. I knew I couldn't explain everything to them all at once, but I had to start somewhere.

"You're right, I know this is hard. It's why I waited so long to tell you. I didn't even tell Jeff right away because I needed to be sure, too. But Mom, Dad, I am sure. I've experienced the grace of Jesus and read the words he spoke in the New Testament, and Jesus is beautiful. He preaches about putting God first in our lives, and loving our neighbor as ourselves, and caring for the widow, and the outcast, and about forgiveness. It's exactly what you taught me to believe growing up! I know our people have suffered greatly at the hands of Christians." I paused and took a deep breath. "But I'm not trying to follow people. People make mistakes. People are human. I don't want to follow people; I want to follow Jesus."

We talked for an hour as I recounted all the miracles I'd experienced since the hallway prayer. Through sniper attacks, Emma's new diagnosis, panic attacks, and even Tom's death, I told my parents about how Jesus had given me new hope and a new life. I apologized for keeping something so big from them for months, and then I told them Emma and I were getting baptized on Sunday. There was another long pause on the phone. I held my breath and prayed that the Holy Spirit would reach through the phone line, wrap around their hearts, and heal the places that hurt. And then they gave me the best gift of all.

"Cara, if this brings you peace and makes you happy, we will find a way to understand it. We just want to be part of your life, no matter what." I whispered a grateful prayer, "Thank you, Jesus."

Chapter Seventeen

A New Life

Sunday Morning, April 27, 2003

Jeff drove us to church that Sunday morning, and everything seemed to shine just a little bit brighter. The sky was a deep, cobalt blue, and there wasn't a cloud in sight. It was the perfect backdrop to the way I felt inside. Before we left for church, I took the wooden cross keychain off my keyring so that I could hold it in my hand all the way to church.

As we got closer to church, I couldn't help but replay every event that had led to this moment, a moment that I was certain God had orchestrated from beginning to end. The Holy Spirit had used Sharon and Rob's everyday, ordinary lives to set off a holy ripple effect that changed the course of not just my life, but Jeff and Emma's too. I hoped that someday, God would allow me to do the same for someone else.

We walked slowly, no ducking, no weaving, heads held high, towards the *Welcome, Everyone* sign. We took up at least three rows, full of Jeff's family and my friends who had come to celebrate our baptism, too. My heart beat loudly inside my chest as the entire congregation stood and sang a new favorite worship song of mine, "This is The Air I Breathe," by Marie Barnett.

And then Brian began his sermon. I tried to concentrate, but my thoughts were focused on what came after the sermon, Communion. Jeff and I still hadn't participated. Now, I felt ready.

A million thoughts ran through my head as Jeff, Emma, and I stood up and joined the hundreds of others moving towards the Communion table. *Did any of the other people know that there was a Jewish woman in line with them? Did they know that the way they lived their life, the way they treated others, and the way they shared Jesus mattered? Did they know that one prayer could change everything?*

As I took the bread and the wine, I hoped Jesus could feel my gratitude, and I prayed that my words and actions would never cause anyone to feel outside of the love of Jesus. Tears of thankfulness and joy welled up in my eyes.

Finally, Brian called us up to the front to be baptized. My heart was beating so loudly, I was certain that the entire congregation could hear. Emma looked adorable in her "scwatchy" white dress, but couldn't contain her nervous energy. She jumped up and down as Pastor Brian, trying not to laugh at her antics, smiled broadly.

"May we all be as excited about Baptism as little Emma Shine is today!" The congregation smiled and laughed, sharing Emma's enthusiasm for what was about to happen.

But the moment I knelt, bowed my head, and closed my eyes, she stopped jumping and stood perfectly still. She placed her tiny hand on my shoulder just like Pastor Brian, Jeff, Sharon, and the other Elders did, and bowed her head to pray over me. I imagined Tom standing next to me, too.

Pastor Brian turned to ask me three questions. "Cara, do you believe in Jesus as your Lord and Savior? Do you intend to be His disciple, and will you be a faithful member of this church?"

Chapter Seventeen: A New Life

"I do," I responded quietly.

"Then, I baptize you in the name of the Father, and of the Son, and of The Holy Spirit." And as the water touched my head, I opened my hands to receive the blessing and whispered the Hebrew phrase I'd been preparing for this moment, "*Hineni*, Lord, *Here I am*." I stood up, a new life bursting from inside my heart.

When it was Emma's turn, she bowed her head, closed her eyes, and then immediately opened one to look at me sideways. She didn't want to miss any of the action. The congregation giggled again, but as soon as Pastor Brian baptized her, "In the name of the Father, and of the Son, and of the Holy Spirit," she jumped back up, clapped her hands, and grinned. The congregation stood and came forward to welcome us with open arms.

Jeff hugged Emma tightly and whispered to me, "I'm so proud of you."

Pastor Brian stood off to the side to give us room, but I made sure to give him a hug, too.

"Well, how do you feel?" he asked, grinning.

"Complete," I smiled. "Just like the verse from John 1:1-17, 'For the law was given through Moses; grace and truth came through Jesus Christ.'"

He teared up, "Exactly, Cara. Well done. Now go share the gift of grace with everyone you meet."

But out of the corner of my eye, I caught Emma suddenly dart off through the crowd, running at full speed. I yelled for her to stop, but she seemed fixed on an invisible target. I ran after her. She came to an abrupt stop, and I quickly realized why she'd been running. Sheku had come after all.

Emma jumped into her arms and gave her a big hug, "Shekwwwuuu! Woook at my dress!"

"Oh, my darling, you look so pretty!" she beamed, giving Emma her biggest smile. I was so grateful that she'd come after all.

"Were you here the whole time?" I asked, wondering if she'd heard all of Brian's sermon on my favorite verse from the Book of John. "A new command I give you: Love one another. As I have loved you, so you must love one another. By this everyone will know that you are my disciples, if you love one another." (John 13:34-35 NIV)

"Yes, I heard it all," she said quietly. A strange, sad look swept across her face. Was she crying? I felt responsible for putting her faith at odds with my desire to have her at our baptism.

"Oh, Sheku, I'm so sorry. I shouldn't have asked you to come."

But she shook her head. "No, Cara. That's not it. Don't feel bad." And then she reached over to hug me tightly. "I'm so proud of you! And the service was wonderful."

"I should probably head home now," she said. "But I'm glad I came." She pulled away, put Emma back down on the ground, and turned to leave.

"Thank you for coming, Sheku! We love you," I said, hoping she could feel the trueness of my words.

She paused, looked around the room, leaned in to give me one more hug, and then whispered quietly so that no one else could hear, "Cara, I want what you have."

Chapter Eighteen

20 Years Later

Written by the author, Sheku, Sharon, and Rob

Cara:

I've often thought about what my life might look like if my friends hadn't shared Jesus with me. Would I still be suffering from panic attacks? Hopeless and afraid to live the life God gifted me? I'm grateful that I'll never know, because the reality is that they DID, and God has allowed that mustard seed to multiply a thousand times over. Within a year of accepting Jesus into my life, Riverside Church needed a Director of Children's Ministry, and although I was still learning the New Testament, Pastor Brian and the rest of the church gave me room to grow and learn alongside the thousands of children who came through our doors over the next twenty+ years.

Every time I worried that I wasn't equipped to step further into ministry, God gave me a sign, as clear as a WVU-TM license plate. Today, the fear that used to paralyze me enables me to serve others who also suffer from anxiety. Through the power of the Holy Spirit, God has given me the strength to share my faith story as a Lay Pastor, Bible study teacher, speaker, and now author. My parents come to church whenever I get the opportunity to teach, and my dad recently bought his first Bible. And I carry extra wooden keychain crosses with me wherever I go, just in case the Holy Spirit allows me to share the gospel the way it was lovingly shared with me.

My journey hasn't always been perfect, and I've made many mistakes along the way. Just like the rest of us, I've lived through many other dark seasons where anxiety, fear, and even doubt threatened to steal my joy. But, just like this story, my need for a Savior only helped me to draw closer to Him. I think that's what James meant when he said, "Consider it pure joy, my brothers, whenever you face trials of many kinds, because you know that the testing of your faith develops perseverance." James 1:2-3(NIV) In my darkest seasons, Jesus was always near.

None of that would have happened if my friends hadn't "set the table" and prepared a place for me. Simply by surrendering their everyday, ordinary lives for Christ's purpose, they showed me who Jesus was, long before I read any of His teachings.

If you've ever wondered about how to share the gospel with those around you, let me encourage you to do three things. First, and most importantly, reflect on your prayer life. Many times, our daily prayers are focused heavily on the wants and needs of our family and friends. But what if you began praying for people that you haven't even met? What if you spoke the Hebrew word *Hineni* meaning, *"God, Here I am,"* and then simply opened your eyes and hearts to those around you? Begin by asking God to humble your words before you speak and imagine what you might say to someone who is thirsting for Living Water. Prepare your heart and your words beforehand and ask God to anoint them with love, not judgment. Let them meet the Jesus who washed feet through the lens of the way you live your life, and let your words reflect that love.

And remember, sometimes the best way to introduce Jesus to others is simply to share what God has done in your life.

Secondly, learn to listen. Chances are, there is someone in your community, at work, in the everyday patterns of your life, who could really use someone to simply listen to them. Listen without an agenda, listen to grow your own understanding of their viewpoint of the world, and listen from a place of humility. No one has ever met Jesus from a place of shame, and compassion for what others are going through is the steppingstone to healing scars.

And thirdly, surrender the outcome. Not every mustard seed will grow, and only God has the power to change hearts, but nothing can grow if nothing is planted. The obstacles that you are placing in front of God's purpose all need to be surrendered. Lay down your fear of rejection or inadequacy and offer the same grace that was gifted to you, to the world.

Pray, listen, surrender, repeat.

And if you're curious about what happened to Sheku, Sharon, and Rob, well, read on. I'll let them tell you themselves…

Sheku:

As I watched Cara journey with Christ, I quietly envied her courage. There was something steady and fearless about the way she pursued truth — how she stepped beyond the safety of childhood religion and cultural expectations to seek a real, living relationship with Jesus. I admired her. But deep inside, I never imagined that path could be mine. I certainly couldn't picture myself being brave enough to openly follow Jesus. Not publicly. Not boldly. The cost felt far too high.

I knew that following Christ out in the open would bring consequences. It might fracture my marriage. It could ripple into my children's lives. I feared being misunderstood, rejected, or even shunned by my own family. And so, I lived quietly, holding my faith like a hidden treasure — close to my heart but behind closed doors.

But even in that hidden place, Jesus met me.

I would pray late into the night, *Jesus, as You have saved me, save my marriage.* Please, don't let my faith be the thing that tears my family apart. And at the same time, I would whisper another prayer — one I barely had the courage to say out loud: *If you ever open the door, I promise I will walk through it. No matter what it costs. Just help me be brave.*

For a long time, there was silence. Waiting. Learning. Growing in the shadows.

And then, one ordinary day, everything changed. He opened the door.

I didn't hear a booming voice or see a burning bush, but His presence was unmistakable. I sensed His whisper deep in my spirit: *Hold My hand. Walk with Me. I will never forsake you.*

That was the beginning of a new kind of life.

Walking through that door meant stepping into risk, into

unknowns — but also into unimaginable peace. It was not without pain. Some fears became reality. There were tears, long nights, and moments where everything felt fragile. But He never left. Not once.

Through every valley, Jesus carried me.

Through every loss, He comforted me.

Through every uncertainty, He faithfully provided.

And through it all, He loved me — not because I was bold or strong, but because I belonged to Him.

Today, my life is simple. It's quieter than it used to be, but richer than I ever thought possible. The blessings I now walk in are not loud or flashy, but they are deep. I've known provisions I didn't deserve, peace I couldn't explain, and joy that didn't depend on my circumstances.

I look back not with regret, but with awe. The same Jesus I once followed in secret is the One who walks beside me now — in the open, in the light, in freedom.

Over my heart, I carry a sacred reminder – a cross tattoo that reads, *Set Free*.

And to anyone who feels the weight of fear, who wonders if the cost is too high to follow Christ with your whole heart — I understand. But I can also promise you this:

Whatever you give up, He repays with His presence.

Whatever you lose, He fills with His deep relentless love.

And wherever He leads you, He will walk beside you. Always.

-Sheku

Sharon:

Algonkian Elementary was a very special school, and I was placed there as a teacher at a very specific and meaningful time in my life. I truly believe God was laying the path for me to grow my faith.

The school had opened just a year before I was hired, and the staff and administration were like no other. We became a family almost instantaneously, and at the heart of it all, was a God-centered focus that Rob nurtured in all of us. As we got to know one another, a small group of us formed a Bible study that met in one of our homes. That group deepened our connections, and soon it expanded into a larger Bible study held in one of the classrooms after school.

Truth be told, I was raised attending church on Sundays, but for much of my life, faith didn't follow me past the sanctuary doors. As parents, my husband and I agreed that going to church was the "right thing" to do for our daughters, but it wasn't until I began studying His Word with the women at school that it all changed for me. I began to crave His word daily, which is why I had a daily desk devotional on my desk. I had no idea that it would lead Cara to Jesus!

When Cara approached me during the chaos of the sniper attacks and asked why I wasn't scared, my response came naturally: Because I have Jesus in my life.

Cara has become a lifelong part of my journey. We often refer to each other as Yin and Yang. In her book, Cara shares how God used me—and a simple desk calendar with daily scripture—to introduce her to Jesus. But let me be clear: this wasn't about me. God allowed me to be in that hallway, and in Cara's life, and my greatest joy has been to watch Him be Glorified in it all.

-Sharon (aka Yang)

Chapter Eighteen: 20 Years Later

Rob:

"And we know that for those who love God all things work together for good, for those who are called according to his purpose." (Romans 8:28 ESV)

I believe that Cara's love story with Jesus began long before the snipers came onto the scene. My role in that story began when I heard God call me and my family to leave the community we loved and move to Northern Virginia to pursue a principalship in Loudoun County. I was certain that this was a new mission field of God's choosing.

Shortly after arriving at Algonkian Elementary School, a parent revealed to me that she and other parents had been hoping for a Christian principal, and began prayer walks around the outside of the building.

To this day, I am still in awe that God chose me to be that Christian principal and orchestrated a long line of events to bring me to Algonkian. That's where God introduced me to Cara Shine, and He began knitting our hearts together.

It was obvious from the beginning that Cara was an exceptional teacher. I was particularly drawn to her kindness and ability to shower great love on her students. She was good to everyone. I knew there was something very special about her, and I was also aware that she didn't have a personal relationship with Jesus.

In the quiet of an early morning or late in the day when everyone was gone, the Holy Spirit would prompt me to walk the halls of Algonkian and pray over the students, staff, and parents. When I would round the hall near Cara's classroom, I would be drawn inside to lay my hands on her empty desk, praying and asking God to come and fill her heart; that she would invite Jesus in.

In His own way and in His own time, God provided. In Cara's pain, He provided opportunities for her and me to have amazing conversations in my office and in her classroom. A sharing of hearts, melded together by the God of creation, made a kingdom impact at our school.

This impact brought a momentum to Algonkian where God was loved, shared, and relied upon for wisdom, strength, and protection. He hand-selected a group of people together for His purpose to create His school where He would be honored and worshipped. As the appointed leader at this school, I relinquished all control to Him and, through His great love and direction, we were empowered to care for the children in our community.

Cara's transformation as a child of God is beautiful and unique. Her daily desire is to lead others to our Savior, Jesus Christ. How that must make our Savior smile.

God does indeed work all things together for His good. Turning two snipers into a miracle of salvation is no exception. To Him be all the glory!

-Rob

Resources

Federal Bureau of Investigation. (n.d.). Beltway snipers. FBI. https://www.fbi.gov/history/famous-cases/beltway-snipers

Beltway sniper attacks. (n.d.). Encyclopedia Britannica. https://www.britannica.com/topic/Beltway-sniper-attacks

National Museum of Crime and Punishment. (n.d.). The Washington, D.C. sniper. Crime Museum. https://www.crimemuseum.org/crime-library/mass-murder/the-washington-dc-sniper/

> If you or someone you love is suffering with depression or anxiety, seek help.

American Association of Christian Counselors: https://www.aacc.net/

About the Author

Cara Shine is a lay pastor, author, speaker, and retired elementary school teacher with a testimony shaped by both deep wounds and unexpected grace. Raised in the Jewish faith, Cara spent much of her early life feeling judged by the Christians around her, experiences that left lasting scars and shaped her understanding of faith and belonging.

Everything changed in the fall of 2002 during the three-week reign of fear surrounding the Washington, D.C., sniper attacks. As a young mother and schoolteacher overwhelmed by anxiety, Cara encountered Christians who reflected the heart of Christ not through judgment or religious posturing, but through love, kindness, and courage.

That season marked the beginning of what Cara describes as a "holy ripple effect," one that transformed her faith, her calling, and her purpose. Today, she is passionate about helping others understand what authentic Christianity looks like when it is lived out with compassion, humility, and grace.

www.ingramcontent.com/pod-product-compliance
Lightning Source LLC
LaVergne TN
LVHW060049250226
832502LV00019B/2084